THE BASICS OF
CHURCH PLANTING

By

Bob C. Green, D.Min.

Copyright May, 2015
by Bob C. Green D.Min.

All rights reserved. No portion of this book may be reproduced, stored in a retrieval system, or transmitted in any form or by any means – electronic, mechanical, photocopy, recording, or any other – except for brief quotations in printed reviews, without the prior written permission of the publisher.

All Scripture quotations are from the Authorized King James Version, Copyright © 1989 Thomas Nelson, Inc.

Published
August 8, 2020

ISBN: 978-1-7351454-5-7

**THE OLD PATHS PUBLICATIONS, INC.
142 GOLD FLUME WAY
CLEVELAND, GA, USA 30528**
TOP@theoldpathspublications.com
www.theoldpathspublications.com

DEDICATED TO:

PATSY, SUSAN, AND TIM

PREFACE

Planting Indigenous Churches

Churches that are established following the **biblical pattern** set forth by the Apostles and first century missionaries will manifest **"indigeneity."** The term "indigenous" is a biological term used to describe a plant that thrives in a specific environment, type of soil, in a given location or climate. At present time there is much lip service given to the starting and establishing of "indigenous churches." Unfortunately many times even those most adamant about this principle and philosophy, in every day practice undermine or violate the principle as set forth in Acts 14 and Ephesians 4:10. The failure to follow biblical guidelines and patterns has led to the establishment of mission churches that are not self-governing, self-supporting or self-propagating. Churches started and established according to New Testament teachings will be able **to exist and flourish without the foreign direction, subsidy and propping up which characterizes mission churches on so many fields.**

The missionary church planter needs to **beware of doing for the national church what they should do for themselves through faith in God**. Rapid results are often obtained through the utilization of **artificial means and short cuts** but in the long run irreparable damage can be done to the establishment of a truly indigenous church. The missionary must **avoid "perpetuating" his ministry.** He would do well to communicate from the beginning that his objective is indigeneity. He must serve and teach in such a way that the nationals participate in the decision to implement indigenous principles. He can thus cause the nationals to develop a sense of "ownership" over the decision to be indigenous or autonomous. Never is a second thought given to the possibility

PREFACE

of churches planted in America becoming "autonomous." New American churches are expected to be autonomous and stand on their own at some point. **Why are churches planted in the rest of the world seen to be any different?**

The keys necessary to the establishment of a truly indigenous church are held by the missionary church planter and the nationals.

1. **The missionary church planter must be a soul winner and must train his converts to be soul winners** (Ephesians 4:10-12). The church planter may be "a one man team" in the beginning of his church planting ministry. This situation may be avoided if he is fortunate enough to have assistance from another church in the area. He will certainly be the Captain of the team until he can train and prepare others to lead in the soul winning efforts (II Timothy 2:2). As he wins souls and trains those he has won to become soul winners the team will grow and new team Captains will immerge.

2. **The church planter must "make disciples" or teach his converts the truths of God's Word.** Spiritual growth and maturity necessary for their lives is the **objective**. The teaching of Bible doctrine is the **means**. The **result** will be the strengthening of the congregation with an eye toward organization and establishment and the day that the missionary can leave to begin another church.

3. **The church planter must train others to "make disciples."** The church planter needs the help of others and the people of the new church need these opportunities to prepare for when he will no longer be present.

4. **The church planter must <u>teach and train maturing disciples that can assume roles of leadership</u>** (teachers, ushers, deacons, nursery workers, department leaders, treasurer, etc). **It is vital to communicate one's heart to these individuals.** This is what Jesus did as HE prepared the Disciples during His three year earthly ministry. The church planter must pray to the Father in Heaven and ask that the Holy Spirit give to them the same biblical vision and passion for the work of the Lord Jesus Christ.

5. The leaders must be taught, <u>**trained by allowing hands on practice**</u> (even if the missionary can do it better he must allow them to gain experience), <u>**entrusted with the work,**</u> (even if they make mistakes) **and then <u>commended to the Holy Ghost,</u>** who alone can do the necessary work in their hearts. Needless to say much time will be spent in prayer for these folk. These leaders will make mistakes... but which of us hasn't? Pour your heart and life into them. Show them that you love them and have confidence in them. When a missionary doesn't trust the national, the national doesn't trust the missionary. The same can be said concerning respect.

6. **The leaders that have God's call on their lives for the ministry will need more extensive training** so they can serve as pastors, evangelists, teachers in the Bible Institute or Seminary and missionaries. This need can be met by the establishment of a Bible Institute in the church. In order for the new church to be fully indigenous it will need a national pastor or pastors (Acts 14:23). Ideally the Bible Institute will continue to function after the church planter has moved to a new location. The missionary might continue to be involved

with the Institute in a teaching role, recognizing the potential for additional laborers for new ministries.

7. **When a congregation has sufficient number of faithful** (faithful in each of the vital areas of membership such as holy living, attendance, financial support, etc.), **biblically knowledgeable, spiritually maturing members it can be organized and "commended to the Lord Jesus Christ."** The "sufficient number" may vary by field. A tribal village congregation would certainly not require the same amount of structure and organization as a congregation in a large metropolitan area. Once the missionary church planter has led the church to this stage, he should step back and move on and recognize the fact that this is now an independent, autonomous, New Testament Baptist church not belonging to him, a mission agency, or association of churches, but to the Lord. The missionary has reached his objective.

Note: A good policy to live by as a church planter is: **"Never invest anything in the establishment of a new church from which you are not willing to walk away.** This policy will keep one from retaining unscriptural power over the local church.

To recognize the supreme role of the Holy Spirit in the entire process of planting churches (evangelism, making disciples, training leaders, maturing the believers), to learn to trust the Spirit's work in and through the new believers, to be willing to step away and relinquish leadership responsibilities and to promote a healthy independency, which should be in reality a dependency upon God taught by the church planter's word and example, from the beginning, requires faith on the part of the church planter. He must recognize the inherent tendency to see weaknesses in others while ignoring his own.

He must remind himself that the Holy Spirit that has transformed him through the Word of God is faithful and almighty to transform peoples of all races, tongues, etc.

In short: Go about your church planting ministry biblically. Partner with the Holy Spirit, trusting Him to do what only He can do, and will do if given the opportunity. **Win, teach, train,** and **trust** the national. Christianize not Americanize. The result should be an indigenous or autonomous (I use the terms interchangeably because in some parts of the world the term indigenous does not give the same connotation) New Testament Baptist church.

TABLE OF CONTENTS

DEDICATED TO: 3
PREFACE 4
   Planting Indigenous Churches 4
TABLE OF CONTENTS 9
COURSE DESCRIPTION 15
COURSE OBJECTIVE 15
   Some questions should we be asking? 16
INTRODUCTION TO CHURCH PLANTING 18
CHAPTER ONE 21
CHURCH PLANTING 21
   Bible Basis: 21
   New Testament Definition: 21
   Practical Definition: 22
   The Origin of the Church 23
   The LORD PROMISES His PRESENCE always. 24
   He promises His PROTECTION 24
   He promises His POWER in verse 49. 25
   Jesus promises His PEACE. 25
   Luke records the progression of the church in Acts chapters One and Two 25
CHAPTER TWO 30
PRE-CHURCH PLANTING MINISTRY CONSIDERATIONS: 30
   THE PERSON: THE CHURCH PLANTER 30
      THE REQUIREMENT OF SALVATION 30
      The requirement of spiritual maturity 30
      NOTE: 33
      NOTE: 35
      Note: Teach "accountability" by being accountable. 37
CHAPTER THREE 44
WHERE SHOULD NEW CHURCHES BE PLANTED? 44
   METROPOLITAN AREAS 46
   THE SUBURBS 48
   THE RURAL AREAS 48
   QUESTIONS 50
   VISIBILITY, access, etc. 52
   For the sake of emphasis: 53
   Illustration: 54
CHAPTER FOUR 56
PREPARATIONS FOR CHURCH PLANTING 56
   Differing Approaches 56
   Differing Forms of Sponsorship 57

THE BASICS OF CHURCH PLANTING

Two Requisites..57
METHODS OF CHURCH PLANTING...58
   The Missionary Church Planter..58
The Advantages of the "Missionary Church Planter" Method........58
The Disadvantages 59
The Pioneer Church Planter 60
Advantages..60
Disadvantages 61
   Note:...62
The Sponsoring Church Method 63
Advantages..63
Disadvantages 64
Variations 65
   The Colonization Model..65
   The Task Force...65
   The Multi-congregational Model 65
   The Satellite Church..65
   The Adoption Model 66
CHAPTER FIVE...67
TEACHING AND PREACHING 67
   PREPARE YOUR PREACHING AND TEACHING MATERIALS BEFOREHAND. 67
   Plan your church program 68
      Sunday School...68
      Worship Services..68
      Training or Discipleship Classes 68
      Teen and/or Youth Activities 69
   PREPARE A CHURCH CONSTITUTION, COVENANT, BY-LAWS, AND STATEMENT OF FAITH 69
   PREPARE PUBLICITY MATERIALS..70
      PREPARE A BROCHURE FOR VISITATION.......................70
      Three things to remember:..71
   DEVELOP A SIMPLE BUDGET 71
      SECURE THE NEEDED OFFICE EQUIPMENT AND SUPPLIES............71
   ARRANGE FOR HOUSING FOR YOU AND YOUR FAMILY 72
   CHOOSE A NAME FOR THE CHURCH 73
   DECIDE ON A SUITABLE MEETING PLACE............................73
      WHEN YOU HAVE A PLACE TO MEET, SET A DATE FOR YOUR FIRST SERVICES 74
      FOLLOW UP ON ALL CONTACTS, MAKE PHONE CALLS, VISITS, WRITE LETTERS, AND SEND EMAILS............................74
   NO AMOUNT OF PREPARATION WILL SUFFFICE IF YOU DO NOT BATHE ALL IN PRAYER. 75

TABLE OF CONTENTS

CHAPTER SIX 77
THE PLAN FOR CHURCH PLANTING 77
   VISITATION AS A TEAM EFFORT 77
   REMEMBER, PEOPLE ATTRACT PEOPLE 78
      IDEAS: 78
      YOU MAY MEET: 79
      EVERY PERSON IN YOUR MINISTRY AREA IS A PROSPECT FOR TRUSTING CHRIST AND ATTENDING YOUR CHURCH -- UNTIL PROVEN OTHERWISE. 79
      YOU MAY OBTAIN PROSPECTS THROUGH: 80
   Note: 82
   detailed preparation for public services 82
   Note: 83
      Make a checklist. 83
      Give thought to: 84
CHAPTER SEVEN 86
REPETITION AIDS IN LEARNING 86
   Building the Church on the Field 86
   Considerations: 88
   KEY NUMBER ONE: 89
   A PERSONAL DAILY WALK with the Lord 89
   The church planter must be a: 91
   KEY NUMBER TWO: 92
   EVANGELISM 92
   Soulwinning……..Considerations: 94
   KEY NUMBER THREE: 97
   Edification, or Instruction 97
   BE A TEACHER 98
   KEY NUMBER FOUR: 100
   Training Leaders 100
   Note: 103
CHAPTER EIGHT 106
THE ORGANIZATION OF THE LOCAL CHURCH 106
   The Charter of the Church 107
   The Church Constitution 107
   The Doctrinal Statement 107
      Charter 109
   Sample Document #1 110
      Church Covenant 110
   Sample Document #2 112
      Membership Covenant 112
   A Sample #3 114
      Doctrinal Statement 114

Sample Document #4 117
   Articles of Incorporation 117
   SAMPLE CONSTITUTION 121
Sample Document #5 129
   Sample Letter Calling for a Recognition Council 129
   Recognition Service 131
CHAPTER NINE **132**
THE ADMINISTRATION OF A NEW TESTAMENT BAPTIST CHURCH. 132
   SET GOALS 133
   Things that help: 134
   Business Meetings 136
      The proper order: 138
   PASTORS and DEACONS 139
   The Duties of a Deacon 143
   CHURCH WORKERS 145
      Guidelines: 145
   THE "TEAM" CONCEPT IN CHURCH PLANTING 146
      Guidelines: 146
   SAMPLE #6 149
      A Leadership Covenant 149
   THE SERVICES OF THE CHURCH 151
      (Worship, Prayer Meetings, etc.) 151
   Note: 152
   Note: 154
   SAMPLE #7 157
      Suggested Guidelines for the Nursery Workers 157
   SAMPLE #8 160
      Suggested Guidelines for the Nursery Leader 160
   SUGGESTED SAMPLE #9 162
      Sunday School Worker's Covenant 162
   SAMPLE #10 164
      A Service Questionnaire for Christian Workers 164
   The Sunday School 166
   SUNDAY SCHOOL TEACHERS 168
CHAPTER TEN **170**
MISSIONS: WORLD EVANGELIZATION **170**
   Developing a Written Church Missions Policy 172
   Note: 175
      THE SENDING CHURCH … 175
      Suggestions for the sending church: 177
Be involved as much as is possible in their ministry **177**
   Note: 181
   A Suggested Missionary Policy 181

TABLE OF CONTENTS

A Suggested List of Items for the Missionary Closet	186
FAITH PROMISE OFFERINGS	188
FOR WORLD EVANGELIZATION	188
HERE'S HOW FAITH PROMISE GIVING WORKS:	189
THE BLESSINGS ARE ABUNDANT	189
WHY SHOULD I MAKE A FAITH PROMISE OFFERING?	190
SAMPLE FAITH PROMISE CARD	192
FAITH PROMISE	192
Hospitality and Missions	193
CHAPTER ELEVEN	**201**
THE LOCAL CHURCH FINANCES & STEWARDSHIP PROGRAM	**201**
Note:	201
A List of Financial Priorities Should Be Established	202
CONSIDERATIONS:	203
CHAPTER TWELVE	**205**
THE CHURCH FACILITIES	**205**
Establish a "Building Fund" account	207
DANGERS:	207
Note:	208
Note:	208
CHAPTER THIRTEEN	**209**
PITFALLS OR DANGERS IN THE CHURCH PLANTING MINISTRY	**209**
Note:	210
Discouragement	210
Burnout	211
The Success Syndrome	211
Note:	212
CHAPTER FOURTEEN	**215**
THE FINISHED TASK: A NEW CHURCH PLANTED	**215**
NOTES:	216
QUESTIONS – STUDY GUIDE	**222**
Chapter One	222
Chapter Two	222
Chapter Three	223
Chapter Four	223
Chapter Five	224
Chapter Six	225
Chapter Seven	225
Chapter Eight…Part One	226
Chapter Eight…Part Two	226
Chapter Eight…Part Three	226
Chapter Eight…Part Four	227
Chapter Nine	228

THE BASICS OF CHURCH PLANTING

Chapter Ten 228
Chapter Eleven 229
Chapter Twelve 229
Chapter Thirteen 230
RECOMMENDED READING: 231
INDEX 233
ABOUT THE AUTHOR: 237

COURSE DESCRIPTION

CHURCH PLANTING is a study of the biblical and practical principles that are basic to the establishment of new local independent Baptist churches.

COURSE OBJECTIVE

The objective of this course is to challenge the student with the commands of Christ so that he becomes involved at some level in church planting, but also to provide biblical guidance and practical information concerning the what, why, where, and how of church planting.

SOME QUESTIONS SHOULD WE BE ASKING?

1. How can we greatly accelerate the beginning of new churches all across America and the entire world?

2. How can we penetrate ethnic America with the Gospel of Jesus Christ?

3. Why is America not seen, by some, as a part of the "Mission Field," a place in which to fulfill Matthew 28:19-20?

4. How can we stimulate vitality among churches that have plateaued, stagnated in growth, or have declined numerically?

5. Have we identified and targeted the needy areas in this country and the world for missionary strategy and action?

6. America is a plural, multi-ethnical, multi-cultural, diverse, perverse, openly pagan, secular society. What implications are there for "strategy"?

7. Is the goal of church-planting efforts world-wide the propagation of churches that have a form of "middle-class American Christianity" or the fulfillment of the Great Commission?

"The fruit of the righteous

is a tree of life:

and he that winneth

souls is wise."

Proverbs 11:30

"I must work the works of him that sent me, while it is day: the night cometh, when no man can work."

John 9:4

INTRODUCTION TO CHURCH PLANTING

There are numerous biblical principles necessary to the process of planting and growing strong indigenous or autonomous New Testament Baptist churches.

A. Local N.T. Baptist Churches should be at the center of all church planting activities, both domestic and foreign.

Established **churches** should be involved directly and indirectly in the **starting and the establishment of new churches**. Churches that follow the New Testament example (Acts 13; Phil. 4) will share their resources, both human and financial. They will **send forth** their members with their **guidance, encouragement, prayers, and finances**. As the late missionary statesman **Dr. Ray Thompson** has said so often:

> "The mission of the church is missions and the mission of missions is church planting."

B. The places and peoples targeted for church planting activities should be selected carefully and prayerfully. The Apostle Paul reveals a guiding principle in his church planting missionary ministry in the words of Romans 15:20. **He sought to preach the gospel where Christ had not been named, or in essence where there was not a gospel preaching church.** Because the gospel of Christ is the only way of salvation it only stands that folks must hear the gospel if they are to be saved. Millions live in places having no witness, no preacher, and no gospel proclaiming church. Even in America there are communities without a gospel witness.

INTRODUCTION

C. A point worth mentioning is the **principle taught by the Lord Jesus Christ** in Matthew 10:33. The ultimate form of rejection of the gospel and Jesus Christ is seen in the persecution of His messengers. **Christ states that when people reject the message, the messengers are to "go to another city."** Should we not understand from His statement that He would have us **"continue on"** to places in need of the message? An awareness of the difference in the response to the gospel message of Christ should enable the church planting team to decide wisely in the matter of where to concentrate its efforts. As the Apostles, the modern day church planter needs definite direction from the Holy Spirit in the matter of <u>where</u> to begin a new church. We are talking about response, not rapid results. **There are places in the world that require a special strategy, an underground church.**

D. It is also necessary that the <u>**message be communicated effectively.**</u> **The message, God's Holy Word, is eternal and unchanging** but the means of communication can vary to insure relevance. The early church planters **preached** (Acts 2), they **taught,** they gave **witness** to individuals (Acts 8), at times their style was that of **proclamation,** at other times it was **apologetic** (Acts 17). The gospel messenger must give consideration to the culture, language, religious environment and other factors in seeking to win souls and establish new churches. **Above all else the message should be presented with Holy Ghost power.**

E. Acts 14:21-28 gives a pattern for church planting. The initial activity was <u>**evangelism.**</u> In verse 21 we are told the Apostles "preached the gospel to that city." The gospel is the message necessary to salvation. The church planter as a soul winner presents to the lost the three main points of the gospel each time he witnesses. The Apostle Paul, under divine direction and inspiration, outlined the points of the gospel in I Corinthians 15:1-4. It goes as follows: **Christ died for our**

sins according to the Scripture, He was buried, and then **He arose after three days, according to the Scripture.** This is the basic gospel message.

In verse 21 we are also told that they **"taught many."** This is the "teaching" aspect of church planting. **The church planter must "make disciples" by the teaching of the Word of God.** It is by these efforts that the new believers are edified and begin to mature spiritually. Thus far the sequence found in these verses is that of evangelism or soul winning and the making of disciples.

The third aspect of church planting is that of **training leaders.** This is seen in verse 23. The church planter should balance his time and energies between soul winning, making disciples, and the **training of the members of the congregation so that they can assume places of service and leadership.** The Lord Jesus Christ commands us to "teach them to observe all things whatsoever I have commanded you" (Matthew 28:19-20).

The local congregation involved in "church planting" and the pioneer missionary church planter alike will do well to follow this biblical pattern. The course of study in this syllabus will emphasize this pattern and hopefully provide valuable information for the accomplishing of the goal.

Chapter One
Church Planting

Bible Basis:

The first reference to the CHURCH is found in <u>Matthew 16:18</u>.

> *"And I say also unto thee, That thou art Peter, and upon this rock **<u>I will build my church</u>**, and the gates of hell shall not prevail against it."*

Jesus promises **to "build" his church** and that it will be endued with conquering power.

> **THE PROMISE: "I WILL BUILD"**
>
> **THE POSSESSION: "MY CHURCH"**
>
> **THE POWER: "THE GATES OF HELL SHALL NOT PREVAIL..."**

New Testament Definition:

The word **church**, or ***ecclesia***, is used predominately in two ways in the New Testament. It is used about **<u>30 times</u>** to refer to the **universal church**. This universal church is the invisible church made up of all believers from Christ's ministry to the Rapture. **<u>The universal church is the Body of Christ</u>** (Ephesians 5:29, 30, I Corinthians 12:13).

> *"For no man ever yet hated his own flesh; but nourisheth and cherisheth it, even as the Lord the*

church: For we are members of his body, of his flesh, and of his bones" (Ephesians 5:29, 30).

"For by one Spirit are we all baptized into one body, whether we be Jews or Gentiles, whether we be bond or free; and have been all made to drink into one Spirit" (I Corinthians 12:13).

Ninety times the word church is used to refer to **an assembly of believers in a given locality** (Romans 16:1, Revelation 3:1).

*"I commend unto you Phebe our sister, which is a servant of **the church which is at Cenchrea**..."* (Romans 16:1).

*"And unto the angel of the **church in Sardis**..."* (Revelation 3:1).

Practical Definition:

A LOCAL CHURCH PATTERNED AFTER THE NEW TESTAMENT EXAMPLE IS A BODY OF BELIEVERS, POSSESSING CHRIST AS PERSONAL SAVIOUR, HAVING CONFESSED THEIR FAITH IN CHRIST PUBLICALLY THROUGH BIBLICAL BAPTISM (IMMERSION, SUBMERSION, EMERSION) IN WATER IN THE NAME OF THE FATHER, THE SON AND THE HOLY SPIRIT, BEING UNITED IN FELLOWSHIP BY COMMON DOCTRINE, FOR THE PURPOSE OF WORSHIP, THE OBSERVANCE OF THE TWO ORDINANCES, WATER BAPTISM AND THE LORD'S SUPPER, FOR EDIFICATION AND PREPARATION FOR SERVICE AND WORLD EVANGELIZATION.

The terms **"to build"** or **"to plant churches"** are used in the scripture to refer to the action of beginning and establishing local churches.

CHAPTER 1: CHURCH PLANTING

*"Who then is Paul, and who is Apollos, but ministers by whom **ye believed**, even as the Lord gave to every man? **I have planted**, Apollos watered; but God gave the increase. So then neither is **he that planteth** anything, neither he that watereth; but **God that giveth the increase**"* (1 Corinthians 3:5-7).

*"For we are labourers together with God: ye are God's husbandry, **ye are God's building**. According to the grace of God which is given unto me, as a wise masterbuilder, **I have laid the foundation, and another buildeth thereon**. But let every man take heed how he buildeth thereupon. For other **foundation** can no man lay than that is laid, **which is Jesus Christ**"* (1 Corinthians 3:9-11).

*"Ye also, as lively stones, are **built up a spiritual house**, a holy priesthood, to offer up spiritual sacrifices, acceptable to God by Jesus Christ"* (1 Peter 2:5).

When an individual, such as missionary or church planter, or group of individuals, in a locality where a New Testament Baptist church does not exist, **leads lost people to faith in Jesus Christ as their Lord and Saviour, and** then begin to **teach them and make disciples of the Lord,** the natural result, biblically speaking, should and can be the establishment of **a new local church.**

The Origin of the Church

The Lord gave the Great Commission to His disciples. The fact that it is recorded in all four of the Gospels serves to emphasize its importance.

The most **"Inclusive"** statement of the Commission is found in Matthew 28:19-20.

*"Go ye therefore, and teach **all nations**, baptizing them in the name of the Father, and of the Son, and of the Holy Ghost: Teaching them to observe **all things** whatsoever I have commanded you: and, lo, I am with you **alway**, even unto the end of the world. Amen"* (Matthew 28:19-20).

The expression "all nations" means "all ethnic groups" and is not limited to geographical boundaries.

The LORD PROMISES His PRESENCE always.

The most **"Emphatic"** statement of the Commission is found in Mark 16:15-18.

*"And he said unto them, **Go ye into all the world, and preach the gospel to every creature**. He that believeth and is baptized shall be saved; but **he that believeth not shall be damned**... they shall take up serpents; and if they drink any deadly thing, it shall not hurt them..."* (Believe and be saved, believe not and be condemned).

The Lord gives an emphatic statement concerning the consequences of not believing as does John in 1 John 5:10-12.

He promises His PROTECTION.

The most **"Explicative"** statement of the Commission is found in Luke 24:46-47.

CHAPTER 1: CHURCH PLANTING

*"And said unto them, Thus it is written, and thus it behoved Christ to suffer, and to rise from the dead the third day: And that **repentance and remission of sins** should be preached in his name among all nations, beginning at JerUSAlem."*

Jesus explains the message...repentance and remission.

He promises His POWER in verse 49.

"And, behold I send the promise of my Father upon you: but tarry you in the city of Jerusalem, until ye be endued with power from on high" (Luke 24:49.

The most **"Enabling"** statement of the Commission is found in John 20:21

*"Then said Jesus to them again, Peace be unto you: **as my Father hath sent me, even so send I you.**"*

Jesus promises His PEACE.

The late Dr. Stinnett Bellue (Evangelist) said: "God has given to us the humanly impossible task of evangelizing the world. He has given to us **the *preserved* Word of God** and the ***power* of the Holy Ghost,** thus enabling us to do the task. When all is said and done, and He has, in reality, done the task, He will reward us as if we did it." HALLELUJAH!

Luke records the progression of the church in Acts chapters One and Two.

Initially the **church was composed of 120 Jews**. God's plan was that the feast of Pentecost would be the time for the descent of the Holy Ghost (see Leviticus 23:15-22 for the O.T. typology). The Lord Jesus promised (Matthew 3:11) that the disciples would be baptized with the Holy Ghost (Acts 1:5). Luke records this in Acts Chapter Two. Though verse four makes specific reference to the "filling", it is evident from the passage that the disciples were both "baptized" with the Holy Ghost" and "filled", or controlled by Him (1 Corinthians 12:13, Acts 2:4). The Lord promised to personally begin and establish His church. He did this while still on earth with the Apostles and those followers that made up the **120 in the upper room.**

There may be disagreement concerning the beginning date of the church but: It is extremely important for the church planter to recognize and associate the **BEGINNING OF A NEW LOCAL CHURCH WITH THE PERSON AND POWER OF THE HOLY GHOST.**

The Lord Jesus Christ states in John 16:7-11,

"Nevertheless I tell you the truth; It is expedient for you that I go away: for if I go not away, the Comforter will not come unto you; but if I depart, I will send him unto you. And when he is come, **he will reprove the world of sin, and of righteousness, and of judgment..."**

The Holy Spirit is the one who convicts sinners of their sin, shows them the righteousness of Christ and coming judgment (John 16:7-11). He regenerates by the Word and transforms believers into the image of Christ.

"Except **the LORD build the house,** *they labour in vain that build it..."* (Psalm 127:1).

We see the small congregation of 120 disciples grow in one day to 3120. Even with the new additions, the number is relatively small compared to the estimated 250,000,000 people that populated the world in the first century A.D. There is progress in number but also a progression in other specific areas. The first disciples were **Jews** and only Jews. For Pentecost there were "devout men out of **every nation** under heaven." In addition to serving as a sign gift to later convince the Jews that the Gentiles had truly been saved and accepted by God (Acts 15:8-11), **the gift of tongues was given to solve the problem of the "language barrier"** (Acts 2:8). Language continues to this day as a barrier to the preaching of the gospel to many people.

The amazing fact is that God had brought to Jerusalem **representatives from "all the world" to hear the gospel, to be saved, and to become a part of the Church** at Jerusalem. Soon, most if not all of these multitudes, would return to their lands of origin because of the persecution they would experience in Jerusalem. They took their "faith in Christ" with them (Acts 8:1-4). What is even more amazing is that **local churches were established wherever these first disciples went.**

It seems worth noting that it took between 13 and 14 years after Pentecost for a local church to commission and send its first **official** missionaries. They were sent from Antioch and not from Jerusalem. It has been suggested by Dr. Bellue that their vision and burden for world evangelization had been dimmed by **the multitude** or numbers syndrome, **the material wealth** (Acts 4:32-37) coming into the coffers of the local congregation in Jerusalem, or by the desire to remain where so many **miracles** were being performed (Acts 3:6, 5; 5, 10).

In addition to the **progress numerically**, there was **progress in propagation or the extension of the gospel into new areas.** The Apostles, the first officials of the fledgling

Church, would see changes in their message. They came to understand more clearly the nature of the Church as a new creation composed both of Jews and Gentiles. The conversion of Cornelius forced them (the Apostles) to accept the fact that **all men** could be saved and that salvation is not bound to the keeping of the law or becoming a Jew (Acts 10, 15).

It is in the **Book of Acts** that we find the seed forms of the **church, its organization, officials, ordinances, theology, practice, extension, etc**. Of course, the doctrine of the church is more fully developed in the part of the Scripture known as the Epistles.

The local churches were established first in Jerusalem and then out to the uttermost. Though there is evidence of local congregations being established in places where the Apostles had not been, most of the known world benefited from the church-planting ministry of the Apostle Paul and those who accompanied him(Acts 8:1-4, Romans 16). May we emphasize that the Lord did not send His disciples into the world just to **get people saved**. He sent them with a broader task, the task of **making disciples. This task can best be completed by the establishment of local New Testament Baptist churches.**

The implications of **Romans 10:13-17** can only be implemented in the context of a local church. It should be remembered that "sending" is also a part of this text. **Evangelism without church planting is not Biblical nor does it lead to the self-propagation that is so vital to the continuance of New Testament Christianity**.

> *"For whosoever shall call upon the name of the Lord shall be saved. How then shall they call on him in whom they have not believed? and how shall they believe in him of whom they have not heard? and how shall they hear without a*

CHAPTER 1: CHURCH PLANTING

preacher? And how shall they preach, except they be sent? as it is written, How beautiful are the feet of them that preach the gospel of peace, and bring glad tidings of good things! But they have not all obeyed the gospel. For Esaias saith, Lord, who hath believed our report? So then faith cometh by hearing, and hearing by the word of God." (Romans 10:13-17)

The ultimate goal of the church planter is the establishment of local, indigenous or autonomous, independent, New Testament, Baptist churches.

This means that through <u>soul winning</u> (Psalm 126:5-6, Proverbs 11:30), <u>discipleship</u> (Matthew 28:19-20), and the <u>training</u> of new leaders (2 Timothy 2:2) a new, <u>self-governing</u> (Acts 6:1-7), <u>self-supporting</u> (Acts 4:34, 1 Corinthians 16:1-2, 1 Timothy 5:17), and <u>self-propagating</u> (Ephesians 4:12-13) church is started and established.

CHAPTER TWO

PRE-CHURCH PLANTING MINISTRY CONSIDERATIONS:

THE PERSON: THE CHURCH PLANTER

THE REQUIREMENT OF SALVATION

<u>It would seem unnecessary to mention this point, but the church planter must have total assurance concerning his relationship with Jesus Christ as Personal Saviour</u>. The writer of Hebrews states that believers are to follow the faith of those that have rule over them. If the church planter/pastor is not sure and secure in his faith neither will his followers be. **The assurance of salvation comes when one believes what God says in His Word**. <u>One knows that he is saved because God's word says so (1 John 5:9-12, Romans 10:13,17).</u>

> *"These things have I written unto you that believe on the name of the Son of God; that **ye may know that ye have eternal life**, and that ye may believe on the name of the Son of God."* (1 John 5:13)

THE REQUIREMENT OF SPIRITUAL MATURITY

> *"Not a novice, lest being lifted up with pride, he fall into the condemnation of the devil." (*1 Timothy 3:6)

> *"Let no man despise thy youth; but be thou **an example** of the believers, in word, in*

CHAPTER 2: PRE-CHURCH PLANTING MINISTRY CONSIDERATIONS

conversation, in charity, in spirit, in faith, in purity."
*(*1 Timothy 4:12)

Note: A simple outline for preaching this verse is as follows: 1) Be an example in conversation (word); 2) In conduct (conversation); 3) In charity (love); 4) In Spirit control; 5) In confidence (faith); 6) In chastity (Purity).

The term "**elder**" (1 Timothy 5:17) implies a mature individual. Paul, inspired by the Holy Ghost, wrote to Timothy and Titus concerning God's standard for pastors, elders, and bishops. It can be concluded from the teachings of a passage such as Acts 20:28 that these three titles are used interchangeably to refer to the same individuals. The titles describe three different aspects or responsibilities of the office of pastor in the local church.

*"Take heed therefore unto yourselves, and to the **flock**, over the which the Holy Ghost hath made you **overseers**, to feed the church of God, which he hath purchased with his own blood."* (Acts 20:28)

A **pastor** cares for the **flock**. (Dr. John Wilkinson, Pastor, First Baptist Church of Hammond, Indiana has stated that he believes "Pastors should smell like sheep – from associating with his sheep, his congregation.")

An **overseer** is a bishop or administrator.

The mature man is a man of **CONVICTIONS**.

True convictions are beliefs based in the clear, unchanging teachings of God's Holy, preserved Word. In the English speaking world the King James Version of the Bible is this preserved Word of God. Distinction should be made between "preferences" and "true Bible-based convictions." Preferences are often times "cultural"; but biblical convictions transcend time, culture, fashion, locality, etc. One is "of man"; the other is produced by the Holy Ghost in the heart of the sincere, submissive follower of Christ as a result of this belief in God's Word.

A young communist guerrilla fighter once informed me that: "that which is not worth dying for is not worth living for either."

It is easy enough to know the difference between preferences and convictions. Ask yourself, "For which beliefs and practices am I willing to die?"

The **doctrinal statement** that you prepare for your new church **should be a statement of your doctrinal convictions**, formed from the Word of God through the work of God's Holy Ghost in your heart.

> *"And how <u>I kept back nothing that was profitable unto you</u>, but have shewed you, and have taught you publickly, and from house to house...But none of these things move me, <u>neither count I my life dear</u> unto myself, so that I might finish my course with joy, and the ministry, which I have received of the Lord Jesus, to testify the gospel of the grace of God...For I have not shunned to declare unto you <u>all the counsel of God</u>."* (Acts 20:20, 24, 27)

The mature man is a man of **COMPASSION** and love. **HE LOVES GOD FOREMOST**.

> *"Jesus said unto him, **Thou shalt love the Lord thy God with all thy heart**, and with all thy soul, and with all thy mind."* (Matthew 22:37)

> *"And thou shalt love the Lord thy God with all thy heart, and with all thy soul, and with all thy mind,*

CHAPTER 2: PRE-CHURCH PLANTING MINISTRY CONSIDERATIONS

and with all thy strength: **this is the first commandment.** *And* **the second is like, namely this, Thou shalt love thy neighbor as thyself.**" (Mark 12:30-31)

The **SPIRITUALY MATURE** man **loves God** as his first love (compare Matthew 24:12 & Revelation 2:4), but he also **loves people**.

"Hereby perceive we the love of God, because he laid down his life for us: and we ought to lay down our lives for the brethren." (1 John 3:16)

The mature man that would be a church planter must also **love** people.

NOTE:

Some pastors, church planters or ministers **use the ministry to "build the people"** (Ephesians 4:11-13). Other pastors use people to **build his ministry** (1 Corinthians 9:15). The first type is always concerned for the welfare of the people, while the second type is more concerned with his own success.

"For **the love of Christ constraineth us;** *because we thus judge, that if one died for all, then were all dead: And that he died for all, that* **they which live should not henceforth live unto themselves, but unto him** *which died for them, and rose again."* (1 Corinthians 5:14)

Love for Christ and others must be the driving force in the life of the church planter.

Only through the fullness of the Holy Ghost can one love, as he should (Ephesians 5:18, Galatians 5:22, 23). A good practice is to review frequently the teachings of I Corinthians 13 in the matter of how real love is manifested toward others. True love always seeks to benefit the person loved.

The church planter must be **SPIRIT-FILLED.**

To be Spirit-filled is no more and no less than being **controlled** by the Holy Spirit. The church planter must **yield his life daily** to God's Holy Spirit.

The church planter must have **Holy Ghost power** (Acts 1:8). He must be secure in his calling and position and not be in a constant **power struggle**.

NOTE: Compare the difference between Peter and John before they were filled with the Holy Ghost on the day of Pentecost and how they were afterwards (John 20:20-21, Acts 3). Before they were filled with the Holy Ghost they were at odds with one another and often critical of one another.

The church planter must seek Holy Ghost **direction** in the ministry, in his messages, methods, etc.

He will seek Holy Ghost **teaching** in his own life but also in the lives of his people (John 16:13-14).

He will look for Holy Ghost **conviction** in sinners (John 16:7-11).

The church planter must be a **SOUL WINNER.**

The Lord promised Holy Ghost power for witnessing to the lost. Planting a new church requires much **soul-winning activity at the commencement and in continuance,** and will only end when the last soul has been won to Christ.

Thirty hours a week of soul winning, as an average, will almost certainly be required in the beginning of a new

CHAPTER 2: PRE-CHURCH PLANTING MINISTRY CONSIDERATIONS

church. **The church planter must be soul-conscious.** He must seek opportunities to share the gospel. There are many theories and types of evangelism but the best of all is to make **aggressive, enthusiastic, compassionate soul winning one's life and life-style.** The Holy Spirit is able to provide the much needed boldness and zeal in the life of the church planter.

The church planter may at times find it necessary to win a person to himself before being able to win the person to Christ. Not every person willingly listens to a stranger present the Gospel, especially if the message is not one with which they are familiar.

The church planter must be a **STANDARD BEARER.**

The church planter, as the spiritual leader of the new church, will have the spiritual and administrative oversight of the flock (Acts 20-28). Leadership abilities will be required. There are good resource materials available. However, our greatest example is the Lord Jesus Christ, and the greatest resource is His Word.

NOTE:

The shepherd **leads** instead of driving his sheep. If folk know how much you care for them and that you honestly seek God's direction in all matters, it will be easier for them to follow you. **Lead by example.**

A true God-called shepherd strives for the welfare and success of the members of his flock. **He finds sweet success for himself in making others a success.**

The church-planting pastor has the obligation and opportunity **to train others** to whom he can delegate responsibilities. The failure to establish an indigenous church on the foreign field as well as in the USA comes, many times, because the church planter fails to:

Train / teach his people. A good administrator (overseer or bishop) seeks to ensure that his followers know **what is expected of them and the "how to" of their responsibilities.**

Transfer to his people the responsibilities, **the freedom, and the authority** to perform the tasks at hand. Often the comment is made by the missionary, "I can do it better, quicker, and with less risk of mistakes, so I'll just do it." If the training has been adequate, give place to your disciples. Which of us can boast of **doing it right the first time, every time** or even after ten times?

Trust his people. **When people sense that the church planter/pastor/missionary, their leader does not trust them, the feeling will be reciprocal.** I believe very strongly that some pastors and missionaries labor for many years in vain to establish an autonomous church because for some reason they project to their people that they are the only one "really" capable of doing the job right. **We must believe that the Holy Spirit can do in their hearts a work equal to,** if not greater than, **the work He has done in ours.** It is exciting to see our disciples surpass us in serving Him effectively. This is real success.

Take stock or **evaluate** the progress being made. A wise practice is to "**look for folk doing a good job at their assigned task or responsibility and reward them with at least a "well done."** If there is a problem, find out where the breakdown is, but remember that your people are learning and also human just like you. Seek to spend more time complimenting the "good" rather than criticizing the "bad." As the late Dr. Lee Roberson often stated, "Everything rises or falls on leadership."

NOTE: TEACH "ACCOUNTABILITY" BY BEING ACCOUNTABLE.

*"Obey them that have the rule over you, and submit yourselves: for they watch for your souls, **as they that must give account**, that they may do it with joy, and not with grief: for that is unprofitable for you."* (Hebrews 13:17)

*"Wherefore we labour, that whether present or absent, **we may be accepted of him**. For we must all appear before the judgment seat of Christ..." 2 Corinthians 5:9-10a*

It is a wise man that seeks counsel of others. The church planter may have most of the answers, but it is almost certain that he doesn't have them all. There may be a pastor friend, a mission director, or some real friend, with whom one can be open and honest. Certainly one's wife should be one's closest friend and confidante. Be certain of the individual with whom you share your doubts, fears, and concerns. Absolute confidence is the key. Do not make everyone or just any "unproven" friend your confidant. You may be courting disaster if that person is a gossip. Pray for God's direction in this matter.

The church planter should be a **<u>STRUCTURED</u> OR DISCIPLINED INDIVIDUAL.**

The church planter keeps his life in order. He **guards his priorities.** A daily list of things to do in the order of their importance is a valuable tool. Use a day planner. Be organized. Daily devotions, which include time in God's Word and prayer, are a must. It is easy for the "good" to replace the "best." Do what you have to do but share responsibilities with new converts.

On the foreign field much time is wasted because missionaries get trapped by menial tasks - (daily trips to the post office box, to the market, etc.). If a missionary church planter has full, support and spends his time doing menial tasks that he could hire someone else to perform for one half or one third the amount that he makes per hour, he is not being wise or a good steward. There is a place for pastor/church planters/missionaries to be involved through manual labor, but consideration should be given to the advice offered by the Apostles:

> *"Wherefore, brethren, look ye out among you seven men of honest report, full of the Holy Ghost and wisdom, whom ye may appoint over this business. But we will give ourselves continually to prayer and to the ministry of the word...And the word of God increased; and the number of the disciples multiplied in JerUSAlem greatly..."* (Acts 6:3, 4,7a)

Could it be that many church planters have gotten sidetracked with the construction of church buildings?

The church planter must be **STABLE EMOTIONALLY, FINANCIALLY, AND IN EVERY WAY.**

The church planter will of necessity **fill the role of pastor** of the new church for a time in the beginning as he starts and establishes the church. Missionaries that will plant churches need to meet the qualifications for a pastor as set down in Scripture.

The list of biblical qualifications for a pastor is found in the third chapter of the Second Epistle of Paul to Timothy. The

CHAPTER 2: PRE-CHURCH PLANTING MINISTRY CONSIDERATIONS

list contains various qualifications that require emotional maturity. The pastor is to be vigilant, of good behaviour, not given to wine, no striker, not greedy of filthy lucre; but patient, not a brawler, not covetous, not a novice.

Very often the ruin of a ministry or failure comes as a result of emotional immaturity in the pastor. It is a sad fact that many a man has failed to reach his full potential because of his own weaknesses. What is even more pitiful is to think that these men often go through life blaming others for their problems.

Sending churches, pastors, and mission agencies play an important role in screening candidates for church-planting ministries. Those involved in the process of screening candidates should keep in mind the words of the apostle Paul as found in 1 Timothy 5:22.

> *"Lay hands suddenly on no man, neither be partaker of other men's sins: keep thyself pure."*

The man, who would be a church planter, or any servant of God for that matter, would do well to seek open and honest input from some godly pastor or friend in the area of "**blind spots.**" We all have areas of weakness in our lives, which for one reason or another are located in a "blind spot." We do not generally recognize these weaknesses. For this reason we need the help of some godly individual who, in Christian love, can point them out to us. Pride would keep us from seeking this sort of help, and it will also cause us to deny that we have a problem.

> *"The way of a fool is right in his own eyes: but he that hearkeneth unto counsel is wise."* (Proverbs 12:15)

> *"Give instruction to a wise man, and he will be yet wiser: teach a just man, and he will increase in learning."* (Proverbs 9:9)

The church planter should **avoid debts** especially when "depreciating" materials or items are involved. Financial instability has caused the demise of many a good work. The words of Proverbs 22:7 are on target when it comes to debt.

> *"The rich ruleth over the poor, and **the borrower is servant to the lender.**"*

The church planter and his family will have to make some sacrifices in order to be in the ministry and start a new church. There must be a willingness to sacrifice. Any sacrifice that might be required of the church planter pales when compared to His sacrifice for us.

> *"For ye know the grace of our Lord Jesus Christ, that though he was rich, yet for your sakes **he became poor**, that ye through his poverty might be rich."* (2 Corinthians 8:9)

> *"For our light affliction, which is but for a moment, worketh for us a far more exceeding and eternal weight of glory..."* (2 Corinthians 4:17)

If at all possible, the church-planter family should be debt free before beginning a ministry. The church planter should also make certain decisions about finances before starting the new church. When making decisions, **every consideration should be given to the importance of safeguarding his personal testimony, as well as that of the new ministry.** Though at first the church planter will have to manage the receiving, receipting, and disbursement of church funds, he should work toward **sharing these responsibilities with other reliable individuals.**

CHAPTER 2: PRE-CHURCH PLANTING MINISTRY CONSIDERATIONS

A workable budget and accurate records, as well as the sharing of financial decision-making, will do much to instill confidence in his leadership. Because of recent abuses by certain evangelists and pastors, the odds are not in our favor. There will always be criticism by some, but we can do much to keep it to a minimum.

The church planter should have stability in his family relationships.

One of the first requirements of a pastor/church planter is that he "be the husband of one wife." Compare 1 Timothy 3:2 with 1 Timothy 5:9. The expression in verse nine concerning the widow, "having been the wife of one man" is the same concept as used in 1 Timothy 3:2 when referring to the pastor. It does not give place to the permissive view of "one wife at a time" or the idea that only the husband or wife at the time of salvation counts. One man suggested that men in America practice polygamy as do the Muslims; only in America they have several wives but just one wife at a time through divorce and remarriage.

Though it is certain that the Lord forgives our past and gives us "new life" when He saves us, it is also certain that He does not wipe away the scars or erase completely all our past... our children are still our children, our financial obligations continue, our diplomas are still valid, etc. Preachers must guard against catering to a permissive society.

The church planter does not necessarily have to be married. Paul the Apostle was most likely a widower. A single man that wants to begin a new church or even pastor an established church will have obstacles to overcome that will require special wisdom and grace.

The oneness that exists between a man and his wife is the greatest testimony they can have concerning Christ and His oneness with His Bride, the Church. According to the teachings found in Genesis 3, Matthew 19:5, and Ephesians 5:25-32, it was from the beginning and continues to be the will of God, that one man and one woman become husband and wife until death do them part. **It was only because of the hardness of their hearts that Moses allowed them to give a bill of divorcement.** As ministers, we must be compassionate and sensitive toward the needs of folk around us, but we must not weaken the church by lowering the standards. Folk are forced to "come up" to God's standard unless we compromise. Some folk have limitations and cannot fill certain positions, but **all can serve God in some capacity.** Young people coming along must see steadfastness in their leaders in these matters.

There is much truth in what I heard as a young preacher. What one generation permits as the exception to the rule, the next generation will practice as the rule.

A church planter needs to **"supply" for his family.** If he loses his family he loses his ministry. Strong families make for a strong church. Many people around the world are desperate for help with their families. Though clothed in human flesh, the pastor and his family can be a model of what a Christian family can be and **offer hope to others.**

The church planter should be **PREPARED.**

Scripturally. Know what you believe. Preach the Word. The Word is "the power of God unto salvation." The Word will set people free. It will feed them. It is the foundation. **The Bible should be the only basis for our faith and practice.**

CHAPTER 2: PRE-CHURCH PLANTING MINISTRY CONSIDERATIONS

Practically. The church planter should have training concerning church planting and church growth.

In Cross-cultural Ministry. Even in the USA, our JerUSAlem, it is becoming more and more necessary to have cross-cultural communication skills to be effective in church planting and pastoring.

Formal education, as well as practical training (gained by experience, serving an internship under the direction of a godly pastor, etc.), are tools that allow the God-called, Holy Ghost-filled church planter great advantages. <u>One can only lead others to his own level of knowledge, experience, and commitment.</u> When one stops learning, he begins to stagnate.

CHAPTER THREE

WHERE SHOULD NEW CHURCHES BE PLANTED?

The will of God is that all believers be involved in the spreading of the gospel and the establishment of new churches. Though we are individuals and members of autonomous churches, we should not be disconnected from the corporate body, the Church of the Lord Jesus Christ. Our individuality and independence should be strengths and not the hindrances that they often are. It is evident that instead of pooling our resources (human, material, financial, etc.) for the great task before us, we "puddle" them. <u>Every God-given resource should be channeled to the task of reaching the world for Christ.</u>

Many Christians and churches are kin to the two and one-half tribes of Israel (Numbers 32:1-23) that found their inheritance on the eastern banks of the Jordan River. If it had not been for God's insistence that they go over and help conquer the land, they would have been content to remain behind and allow the remaining ten tribes to fend for themselves.

> *"Wherefore, said they, if we have found grace in thy sight, let this land be given unto thy servants for a possession, and bring us not over Jordan. And Moses said unto the children of Gad and to the children of Reuben, Shall your brethren go to war, and shall ye sit here? And wherefore discourage ye the heart of the children of Israel from going over into the land which the LORD hath given them?"* (Numbers 32:5-7)

CHAPTER 3: WHERE SHOULD NEW CHURCHES BE PLANTED?

Not only were they needed as participants, as each of us are in matter of world evangelization, but by absenting themselves, they would "**discourage**" those that were going to battle. A person can only be in one place at a time, but we can certainly ask God for a world-wide vision and do all that we can to assist those laboring in other areas. Much of what is needed to make the difference in evangelism and church planting around the world is stockpiled in churches in the Bible belt. This is obvious as one evaluates personnel and possessions.

Consider this:

Between Washington, DC, and Boston, MA, there are approximately <u>120 million people</u>. This is one third of the population of the USA. There are only about <u>150 fundamental Baptist churches in all that area</u>.

In the Chattanooga, TN. area, there are over 300 Baptist churches. In Winston Salem, NC, there are 200 plus Baptist churches. Is God not concerned about the millions that have no church? Would He not have someone go to them with the gospel? Is our burden really for His will, for the lost, or is it for a "comfort zone"? We must practice Romans 15:20.

> *"Yea, so have I strived to preach the gospel.* **Not where Christ was named,** *lest I should build on another man's foundation..."*

We would do well to regularly ask ourselves how we are doing in carrying out the command of Christ. As local churches, we should concentrate our efforts in the part of the field that has fewer labourers.

Basically, the world can be divided into three areas. These are:

<u>Metropolitan areas</u> (Cities and towns, inner city, etc.)

<u>Suburban areas</u> (areas adjacent to the towns and cities)

<u>Rural areas</u> (country, remote villages, etc.)

METROPOLITAN AREAS

The first local church was in the city of Jerusalem. It was, of course, a population center. From the city the message of the gospel went out to the outlying areas. Later the center of activity moved to another city, Antioch. The Apostle Paul was led by the Holy Ghost to preach and teach in population centers. These cities were strategic because of their location along the thoroughfares of the Roman Empire, but also because of the sheer number of people that could be reached. Paul and his group were able to reach the known world with the gospel by planting churches in Ephesus, Philippi, Berea, Thessalonica, and Corinth. Though several house churches were already established by the time he reached Rome, it is probable that he helped to stabilize them through his teachings.

We would be wise to give greater consideration to church planting needs in the metropolitan areas of the world.

<u>The following are some of the possible reasons why there are not more churches planted in the cities:</u>

- The dangers (crime, gangs, etc.)

- The inconveniences (traffic, housing, poor schools, etc.)

- The cost of living

- The extremely high cost of purchasing or even renting facilities

- Ethnic groups (prejudice, etc.)

CHAPTER 3: WHERE SHOULD NEW CHURCHES BE PLANTED?

- Decaying economies, infrastructure, etc.

- FAILURE TO UNDERSTAND THE HEARTBEAT OF GOD

In some areas, metropolitan churches have moved away from the inner city environment to locations in the suburb. Crime, the arrival of different language, ethnic and cultural groups, the decadence of the infrastructure and the economy are all contributing factors.

Some reasons for planting churches in the city:

- There are millions of people to be reached in a reduced area.

- The cities are centers for communication, education, culture, government, immigration, etc.

- The influences and forces that mold our society are found in the city.

- The gospel is more likely to flow from the city to the rest of the country.

- Suburban churches can minister to the metropolitan areas through extention ministries, etc.

- The simple fact is that Christ is moved to compassion by the multitudes. We should be as well.

THE SUBURBS

Suburbs are the communities that are adjacent to the large cities. There is usually more life or vitality in these growing areas. Those not trapped in the inner city by poverty or other circumstances are moving to the suburbs. One only has to spend some time in the large cities to understand why. The security and slower pace of the suburb is very appealing. Of course, many commute daily from the suburbs to the city because of work or school.

This is also a needy field. A church planter will find some things about the suburbs conducive to the establishment of a typical middle class American church. Often, a new church in the suburbs is able to stand on its own more rapidly. Because people in the suburbs are more mobile, a church there can draw people from a greater distance.

THE RURAL AREAS

It has been estimated that 75% of the churches in America have 75 members or less. This is usually the case with rural churches. As with church planting in any part of the world, there are unique problems and challenges associated with starting a church in a rural area. Often distance, adverse weather and living conditions, isolation, and even clannish attitudes contribute to the difficulties of church planting. Each area will present unique challenges whether the area is in the jungles of South America or the western states of the USA

When praying about where to establish a new church, one should be open to God's direction. He is the LORD of the harvest. When He leads in a specific way and to a specific place, He is able to provide the grace, wisdom, and strength that one needs to work there. Before we move on to some of the specifics for an individual to consider when

CHAPTER 3: WHERE SHOULD NEW CHURCHES BE PLANTED?

determining God's will and a specific place of service, let's reflect on this:

We should **not** start a new church because:

- There is not a church in the area of certain inclination (formal, informal, emotional, different music, etc.)

- There is a need in the life of an individual, a family, or group of individuals to have a church that is "theirs" so they can do things their way.

- One wants a place to preach but doesn't want to move to an area where there is a real need for a church.

- A disqualified preacher or deacon wants to continue in the ministry, etc.

It seems that 99% of the Baptist churches that have been started in the past 50 years have started because of personality conflicts. Very few have begun because of real doctrinal differences or because there was a real need.

Church planting should be done because of His command. Church planting should be done where the Lord of the harvest directs. He certainly will direct those who are listening to the spot in the harvest field where He wants to do a work. Should we consider the "field" that needs to be harvested and also the fields where there will be "gleanings."

Church planting should be done with the goal of reaching as many lost people as possible with the gospel. Worship is integral, and God commands it, but He is not as concerned about us having a "get down" good time as He is about the lost being saved and believers growing in the grace and knowledge of the Lord.

When a man is convinced that God wants him to have a church-planting ministry, he must determine in what part of the world he is to labor. If he is burdened for the foreign field, or for an ethnic group, or even a place in the USA where he will be confronted with the need for cross-cultural communication skills, **he should prepare in certain matters before going to the field.**

The WHERE of God's will can be broken down into <u>what country</u>, <u>what town</u>, <u>city or area</u>, and in most cases, <u>what area in the city or town</u> is to be targeted (that is, where in the city is the church to be established).

QUESTIONS

<u>I suggest that some of these questions are more pertinent than others for selecting a place in which to start a new church</u>. Each question has validity, but at times the decision to work in a certain area hinges on a conviction of God's will and not so much on, "Well, these are all reasons why I believe it is His will for me to plant a church here." Some of the questions asked will help us prepare our hearts for making the decision. Some of the questions cause us to face before hand some of the difficulties we may face, **but it should be remembered that the ultimate decision is one of faith in Him - His direction, and provision, and His working.**

1. Is there a real need?

2. Have you surveyed the particular place personally?

3. Have you discussed your plans with your **pastor**, **sending church**, **mission director**, and others, with whom you counsel yourself?

CHAPTER 3: WHERE SHOULD NEW CHURCHES BE PLANTED?

4. Have you talked with other good pastors in the area where you are praying about working?

5. Do you already have contacts, people that are interested in working with you to begin a new church in that area?

6. Will these folk be a help or a hindrance? It is unwise to begin a new church with "disgruntled" believers.

7. Are you prepared for a ministry in the particular area?

8. Are your wife and family with you in the decision? This is extremely and absolutely important.

9. Has God burdened you for that particular place?

10. Do you want to go to that place? It is valid and reasonable to think that God could want us to work in a place "where we want to work." (Psalm 37:4-5)

11. What is the spiritual condition of the community? Does one religion or another dominate the area?

12. May you even go there? Some hearts are closed doors. Politically some doors are closed. (Muslim countries, Cuba, China). The Lord is the One who opens and closes doors.

13. Is it practical for you to go there? In America, it is very difficult for a white person to have effectiveness among blacks and vice versa. Some Anglos have not been accepted to labor among some Native Americans.

14. Will the area be able to support a church, pastor, etc.?

15. Is the area growing, or does it have a dying economy?

16. What difficulties will you face in acquiring property, housing, and/or a place to begin the church?

This is only a partial list of questions that should be asked. **One must count the cost** (Luke 14:28-30), but more importantly, **one must be willing to pay the cost**. We live in a day when modern transportation and communication and our prosperity make possible a visit potential fields of service before a decision is made about whether one is to serve there. This allows for a good survey trip and, most of the time, for wiser decisions.

Once a decision concerning God's will in the matter of "WHERE" (which country and city, town or rural area) has been reached, then one can more accurately appraise the field. It is often wise to move to the field before pinpointing the exact part of town where the church will be started. Of course, you may begin in one area and later move to another.

If you begin in a village in an underdeveloped country, the situation will be different from locating in a city or even suburban area. You will not have trouble being identified. In most cases, the success of a new church will depend on three things.

VISIBILITY, access, etc.

Be visible to the community and locate an area that has easy access (not on a dark, dead end street where folk are afraid to attend). Being visible also means that you make people aware of your presence through visitation, announcements, etc., but for now we are more concerned with the location. Of course, your location will determine whether you have to begin in a home, possibly in a storefront, a rented building such as a school, funeral home, lodge, union hall, or even a church of another denomination that is willing to rent.

CHAPTER 3: WHERE SHOULD NEW CHURCHES BE PLANTED?

You may be fortunate enough to have access to an abandoned church building. A church-planter friend of mine rented a large airplane hangar in which to begin the new church.

Make your location **PRACTICAL**, as **COMFORTABLE** as possible and nice (clean, orderly, etc.). In a village, just a plank or a log may be sufficient to make a pew, but in all circumstances, you will need to strive for a good impression.

For the sake of emphasis:

In planting a church or growing a church, there are some key elements. We find some of these in Mark 3:1-12.

The multitudes came because of the following:

1. **Jesus' presence**

2. "And again he entered into Capernaum after some days; and it was noised (announced, it was known in the community) that he was in the house...And straightway many were gathered together..."

3. **Jesus' preaching**

4. "and he preached the word unto them"

5. **Jesus' provision of their needs**

6. "...Son, thy sins be forgiven thee."

The church planter starts by getting the word out, and **the location will have much to do with whether people know he is there** or not. It is difficult to move a church from the lower class section of town to a higher classes section. Lost people don't usually gravitate to a class lower than their own. The "cheap building" you rent to start may end up costing you too much. If you target a low-income area, you must be prepared to spend more time establishing the church because it will take longer to reach the "self-supporting" stage. If you target a middle-income area, you will probably be able to reach both upper and lower class sections. "Targeting" is not "discrimination"; it is simply a strategy. **Saved people accept the idea of integration and equality more readily** than lost people do. At least, that is the way it should be.

Illustration:

In 1970, with the Bruce Bells, and the Roland Garlick family that had actually invited us to help them start the church, we began the first church in all of Central America with an outreach to the middle and upper classes. We were criticized for targeting these folk and accused of discrimination. We did not turn anyone away; we simply concentrated our visitation in the middle class subdivision where a house had been rented. In the first three months, we saw the Lord save folk who were doctors, lawyers, dentists, university professors, architects, high ranking military officers, maids, nannies, construction workers, peasants, etc. At one time, we had a person who lived in a stick hut sitting in the same pew with the Director of the National Police. The strategy worked.

That church is 50 years old, has a national pastor/pastors and Bible Institute, and has reached out to other communities in El Salvador with the Gospel. The Iglesia Bautista Miramonte averages about 800 in Sunday services. The strategy was that the middle and upper classes would have the education and other resources to reach their own people. They have done this. Between the Miramonte and the Tabernáculo Bautista of San Miguel which the Lord allowed me and Patsy to start in 1973 and has prospered under national leadership, have dozens of daughter churches have been established. As a missionary church planter we were blessed

CHAPTER 3: WHERE SHOULD NEW CHURCHES BE PLANTED?

to see churches we helped plant or planted, planting new churches.

CHAPTER FOUR

PREPARATIONS FOR CHURCH PLANTING

If a man and his family have come to the conclusion that it is God's will for them to be church planters, it means that God has done a work in their lives, and they have made several very important decisions. There have probably been some years of **training and preparation** as well. If by this time they also know where they are going to be working, they are well on their way to one of the most rewarding and challenging areas of Christian service.

Before actually beginning the work of establishing or planting a new church, the church planter should consider and decide on the type or model of church planting he will follow. There are several models from which to choose. Some of these models have proven to be very effective.

Differing Approaches

There are different types of fields. A city ministry would require an approach different from that of a village or rural ministry. Because church planters differ in their personalities, background and abilities they approach church planting differently. The approach that serves one church planter well may not give the desired results to another. If the church planter has the long range goal of establishing a church and becoming the resident pastor of the church he will probably approach his church-planting ministry somewhat differently than the church planter who intends to establish the church and then move on to another location to repeat the process. There are missionary church planters that have started and established a number of autonomous churches in the course of their ministry. A few missionaries have started and established and continued to serve as missionary pastor long term, a central church out of which numbers of additional churches have been established. BIMI missionary, Dr. Rick Martin is one such missionary. The Lord has blessed his church planting ministry with over 500 daughter churches being established in the Philippines. The church planter will find a "method" most suited to his personality, education, spiritual gifts, experience, background and objective or goals and calling. No two men are exactly alike. The key is to be directed by God and effective. In His grace God uses each of us… in spite of ourselves.

Differing Forms of Sponsorship

Some church planters are sponsored by a single church, others serve as missionaries sent by the local church through a missions agency, and still others go as "tent makers" who support themselves through working a secular job. **One fact should remain constant no matter the method and that is that the church-planting ministry should be "<u>from a local church, to a local church</u>."** Churches should be planting churches.

Two Requisites

Is the church planting method **Scriptural**? **The end does not justify the means.**

Does it give Scriptural results? Does it work? Does it work for you?

METHODS OF CHURCH PLANTING
THE MISSIONARY CHURCH PLANTER

The missionary church planter is:

1. A man that is supported as a missionary by local churches and is able to give himself full-time to the ministry.

2. A missionary pastor. He begins the new church and stays long enough to get it established, but he is not a permanent pastor. **He works himself out of a job.** He is a combination of evangelist and the pastor. He evangelizes but also disciples his converts. He must train leaders and work for the day that the newly established church can call a permanent pastor. He must have wisdom to neither leave too soon, nor stay too long. At times especially on the foreign field, the missionary structures the work around himself and thus perpetuates his ministry. This should be avoided.

The Advantages of the "Missionary Church Planter" Method.

1. There is strong, experienced leadership for the new church from day one.

2. He can dedicate his time to the task and thus does not have to divide his time and energies. He can give himself to evangelism and discipleship in the crucial early months of the ministry. He is able to make key visits whenever the opportunity arises and is not bound by a secular job work schedule.

CHAPTER 4: PREPARATIONS FOR CHURCH PLANTING

3. He is accountable to his home church, supporting churches, and missions agency. This provides for sufficient accountability but also allows him to count on the support, advice, and supervision of these same individuals or institutions.

4. The missionary church planter has the prayers and backing of a number of churches. **Prayer is vital.** In some cases, it is an encouragement to young believers to know that they are part of a community of churches.

The Disadvantages

1. If the missionary acts out the role of the "Great White Father," he may cripple and permanently damage the new church. He may fail to train local leaders.

2. If the new church becomes too accustomed to receiving from external sources (missionary's resources) they may not contribute as they should. The new church should be taught financial faithfulness toward the pastor and all the obligations of the church such as supporting missionaries, etc.

3. If the missionary has to leave for periods of time to report to his supporting churches, this is also a detriment. In some cases, the missionary goes to the field before he has adequate support and has to travel every week in order to raise the support he lacks. This is not wise.

4. Raising support can take two years or more. Deputation should be seen as a time of ministry. Some argue that the tent maker can be on the field almost immediately. Many foreign countries do not

allow foreigners to work secular jobs. The full-time missionary only has to raise his support one time. He is free to start and establish many churches in various locations. Usually, as long as the missionary church planter is faithful, he can retain most of his financial support, thus having to raise the bulk of the support only once.

5. Some times the new church reacts to the fact that their beloved missionary is going to move on at some point in time. Sometimes folk hesitate to join a new church if they are aware that the missionary pastor is only temporary.

In the long run the missionary church planter method will give the best results when the goal is to start a number of churches.

The Pioneer Church Planter

The pioneer church planter is not affiliated with any missions agency, and he starts the new church with the intention of remaining permanently as pastor. Usually, any support he receives is temporary. If he seeks financial assistance from churches, it is with the idea that it can be phased out, as the new church is able to take on his salary.

Advantages

1. A pioneer church planter goes to his field and finds a job to support himself, so that he is not delayed by having to do deputation. Some church planters and their families receive special love offerings and support from churches and individuals during the initial stages of their ministry. God honors the pioneer

CHAPTER 4: PREPARATIONS FOR CHURCH PLANTING

church planter's faith. Dr. Wallace Cooley the Pastor of the Liberty Baptist Church in Fort Pierce, Florida is just one example of a pioneer church planter that has been greatly used of God.

2. Usually, a pioneer church planter is self-motivated and an innovator who makes things happen through aggressive evangelism. Dedicated men, not committees, start churches.

3. The people are impacted by the church planter's zeal, faith, vision, and desire to get the job done for the Lord's glory.

4. Under the leadership and following the pioneer church planter's faith, Christian character is built into the congregation as they look to God to obtain property and adequate facilities. This is not to say that the same is not true of the churches built by the missionary church planter, especially if he guards his congregation against the "welfare syndrome."

Disadvantages

At times the pioneer church planter, especially if immature and inexperienced, makes unwise decisions that could be avoided if he were accountable to a sponsoring church or mission agency, or both. **All church planters should be accountable to a sending church.**

1. The pioneer method reflects the strengths but also the weaknesses of the church planter.

2. The needed encouragement that comes from being a part of missions agency is not present.

3. The sacrifices that the pioneer church planter and his family make can be unusual, to say the least.

4. The development of the ministry is slowed because of the demands a secular job can make on the church planter's time and energy.

5. Though the Bible teaches pastoral authority, it does not teach pastoral dictatorship. Because of the strong personality that a pioneer church planter must have and also because of the sacrifices that he and his family make to establish the church, the temptation can be greater for him to see the church as his and not the Lord's. He can become accustomed to making all or most of the decisions, and thus weakens the new church.

NOTE:

I recommend the book written by Dr. Paul Chappell, "Guided by Grace, Servant Leadership for the Local Church." Dr. Chappell lives and teaches by his example the Scriptural truth of servant leadership.

6. The community may react negatively to the pioneer church planter if they see him as coercive or arbitrary (dependent on his own discretion).

7. He may have trouble delegating authority out of fear of losing his control of the ministry. The Holy Spirit can temper the strong personality of the pioneer church planter and use his strengths to establish the new church.

8. The pioneer church planting pastor that supports himself probably does not have the **"PRAYER SUPPORT"** that a missionary that has done "deputation" has.

These dangers exist in other forms of church-planting models, but they seem to be more prevalent in the pioneer method.

The Sponsoring Church Method

The Sponsoring Church Method, also known as the mother/daughter method, is when a single sponsoring church takes members, usually families, from its congregation to form the nucleus for a new church. The sponsoring church not only provides these "ready made members," it provides funds, equipment, counsel, and moral support. A healthy parent church can very well sponsor a number of new churches while continuing to grow.

Advantages

1. The biblical principle of "from a local church to a local church" is seen in this form of spontaneous reproduction.

2. The members of the parent church are actively involved in the establishment of a new congregation.

3. There is, of necessity, motivation to introduce new levels of evangelism, discipleship, and preparation of leaders.

4. This leads to spiritual vitality.

5. The new church has the advantage of "people." People draw people.

6. There is financial stability.

7. Doctrinal stability is apparent.

8. There are mature leader and trained teachers from the beginning.

9. The strengths of the parent church are ensured in the new church.

10. Teams of people from the parent church can assist in special activities (visitation, special services, outings, etc.)

11. The parent church by sending several families to assist in the planting of the new church may be spared the expense of building larger facilities due to overflow crowds.

12. The parent church can be supportive of the new church in the matter of purchasing land and building facilities.

13. The church ministry (evangelization, making disciples, etc.) is "localized." The ministry is taken to the community.

Disadvantages

Except for the fact that some members in the parent church may have fears about losing key members or having competition from a new church, there are very few disadvantages. A wise pastor will prepare the congregation well in advance for any stress that the new ministry might cause.

Note: This method is not practical on the fields where there are no established or mature churches. A combination of pioneer and missionary church planting will have to be done, at first, in order to have churches that are capable of parenting new churches on the field. The church planter whether a pioneer or a missionary should be sent by his home church and the churches he establishes should be considered missions of his sending church.

Variations

THE COLONIZATION MODEL

Members from the parent church move to the new location for the express purpose of helping establish the new church. There may be times when several families already live in a needy community and they agree to leave the established church to become a part of a new congregation.

THE TASK FORCE

The families of the parent church are temporarily on loan to the new church until it can be planted and established.

THE MULTI-CONGREGATIONAL MODEL

The parent church sponsors a number of daughter churches, usually using the parent church's facilities. Each of these new churches may differ in ethnic or cultural origin. New churches could be started to reach the Hispanics, Chinese, French Canadians, the deaf, etc.

THE SATELLITE CHURCH

The parent church sponsors satellite churches or chapels. In some cases, the chapels remain as extensions of the parent church. Some parent churches allow the chapel/mission churches to eventually become autonomous

THE BASICS OF CHURCH PLANTING

churches. In the 1960s and 1970s, under the pastoral leadership of Dr. Lee Roberson and Dr. J.R. Faulkner, the Highland Park Baptist Church of Chattanooga, Tennessee had as many as 100 chapels. I know from personal experience as pastor of the Wayside Baptist Chapel in Sale Creek, TN. that these satellite churches or chapels provided preaching/pastoring opportunities for many of the students at Tennessee Temple. Many souls were saved and many people in North Georgia and Eastern Tennessee were provided with a church to attend.

THE ADOPTION MODEL

This situation exists when a church adopts a struggling church and seeks to bring it to maturity.

There are a number of different methods that are a combination of some of the preceding methods. Remember God uses men to do church planting work. As a man of God, the church planter will decide which of these methods, or which combination of methods will best work for him. **The individual who intends to spend his life planting a number of churches would do well to consider the advantages of being sent out by his home church but also associating with a mission agency.**

CHAPTER FIVE
TEACHING AND PREACHING

Once an individual has determined that God has indeed led him into a church planting ministry, has decided on a church planting method, and chosen a place, he should begin to prepare by attending to several matters. Careful planning will enable him to build a stronger church with fewer surprises and pitfalls.

PREPARE YOUR PREACHING AND TEACHING MATERIALS BEFOREHAND.

This is a wise move because it will free you to simply review the materials before actually using them in your teaching and preaching ministry. This beforehand preparation will allow you to spend more of your time for soul winning and discipleship training. Avoid dry or stale messages, however.

THE SECOND THING THAT MAKES FOR A SUCCESSFUL CHURCH PLANTING MINISTRY IS TO "GIVE THE PEOPLE SOMETHING FOR THEIR SOULS WHEN THEY COME TO YOUR SERVICES."

Your church may be visible and they may come, but if they are not fed spiritually and blessed by having been in the services, chances are they won't come back.

Be sure that each of your messages is packed with dynamic but simple truths from God's Word. You need to preach on such subjects as salvation, the local church, prayer, Bible study, how to witness, stewardship, separation, surrender, service, and the Second Coming. Prepare and preach as if you had hundreds of people in the congregation. If you can't hold those you have, you probably won't get more. Mention the fact that your teaching and preaching are directed at helping the lost to be saved and the saved to grow in the Lord. Share with these new converts the fact that you are working toward establishing a new church and what that means. Don't assume that they know all the basics. Lay a doctrinal foundation both for their lives and the new congregation.

Plan your church program

SUNDAY SCHOOL

1. Number of classes (this will depend on the number of trained teachers you have.)

2. Study materials you plan to use (Have them on hand and obtain discipleship courses if you plan to use them in S.S.)

WORSHIP SERVICES

Have Christ honoring music and special singing if available. Have a service for preaching evangelistically, preferably when you know the unsaved will be present. Be punctual. Be clear in your teaching. Preach the Word. Seek to lead the new church in worshipping the Lord.

TRAINING OR DISCIPLESHIP CLASSES

Train your people to be soul winners. Provide them with the necessary materials (tracts, invitations, Gospels of John and Romans, etc.) Meet weekly with new converts for a regular time of one-on-one discipleship. Prepare materials beforehand. Train the people and get them involved in the discipleship ministry.

CHAPTER 5: TEACHING AND PREACHING

TEEN AND/OR YOUTH ACTIVITIES

The young people that God gives to you will be one of your greatest assets. Refreshments, fun & games, Bible study, and scripture memorization should be a part of youth activities but not necessarily in that order.

PREPARE A CHURCH CONSTITUTION, COVENANT, BY-LAWS, AND STATEMENT OF FAITH

Before you begin the new church, you should have these materials prepared and on hand:

<u>Constitution and By-laws:</u> Most States and foreign countries, in order to allow a congregation to incorporate and hold the status of a non-profit religious organization, require a church constitution. The congregation in order to hold the title-deed to the church's property will need to be incorporated. The constitution should be Scriptural, legal, and workable. It should contain safe-guards against disorder and serve as a guideline for the smooth functioning of the church. Remember, the congregation has the authority to change the constitution if it becomes a burden or impractical.

<u>Covenant:</u> Though most Baptist churches have a covenant on display, very few call attention to it or seek to abide by its principles. It should not be this way. Each person who becomes a member of the church should understand the implications and responsibilities of being a part of the local congregation. Each member should make a commitment to abide by the principles contained in the covenant.

<u>Statement of Faith:</u> This is a statement of the doctrinal position of the church. It should be Biblical and thus it will

reflect the historical Baptist position. All members of the church should know, understand, and adhere to the doctrines of the church.

A word of warning: It is wise to get legal counsel from people and organizations that can give vital information concerning functioning within the law of the land.

PREPARE PUBLICITY MATERIALS

You should have good quality photos of yourself and also of you with your family. Normally, printers request a good color photo, but in the case of color publications, you will need to be prepared. Modern day computers make this a lot easier. Check with the editor of the local newspaper concerning their requirements. There are some newspapers that provide free advertisements for churches.

PREPARE A BROCHURE FOR VISITATION

Since first impressions are very lasting, you will want to have a first-class job done on the printing of these materials. The brochure should be prepared so that you have them to hand out as you start your door-to-door visitation.

Your brochure should include:

The church's name (as a church planter you have the opportunity to choose the name of the new church), address, phone number, FAX number, information that indicates the location of the church, a picture of the pastor with his family, his name, and phone number, the church's email address and webpage. It would be wise to include a schedule of services, services provided (nursery, deaf ministry, bus ministry, etc.), and a brief doctrinal statement. Give a brief explanation of why you are starting the church. A brief presentation of the plan of

CHAPTER 5: TEACHING AND PREACHING

salvation is a very good idea, too.

THREE THINGS TO REMEMBER:

1. Gear your brochure to the lost or unsaved. Use terms they will understand.

2. Design the brochure to stir interest and give an invitation to the people to attend your new church.

3. Give the information that folk will need to know should they decide to attend.

Have plenty of good gospel tracts on hand in addition to the brochure. Make sure that your church is identified on all literature. Make these available to your people and encourage them to help you get the word out. It may also be a good idea to have some inexpensive Gospels of John & Romans available to give out. You will also find those who desire a Bible or New Testament. Bibles can be sold at cost as opposed to just "giving" them away, so that the individual appreciates its value.

DEVELOP A SIMPLE BUDGET

You should have an idea of what the monthly expenses are going to be, as well as the initial expenses to get started (printing, literature, etc.). You can share this information with those who are interested in helping you get started and in praying for you.

SECURE THE NEEDED OFFICE EQUIPMENT AND SUPPLIES

Good office equipment (desktop computer, color printer,

THE BASICS OF CHURCH PLANTING

FAX machine, safe box, etc.) will allow you to work more efficiently. Be practical. Whatever is donated to the church belongs to the church and should remain with the church after you have finished your church planting ministry. Eventually, a multimedia projector, screen, P.A. system, large TV, DVD player, for teaching purposes can be useful.

Hymnbook, visitor cards, offering envelopes, a clerk's book for the minutes taken in the business meetings, a financial ledger for recording financial information, a membership role book, and by all means baptismal certificates will be needed. You may want to give completion certificates to those finishing the discipleship courses. Name tags for ushers, greeters, etc. may be helpful.

ARRANGE FOR HOUSING FOR YOU AND YOUR FAMILY

The main consideration here is for the security and comfort of your family. Their happiness will mean much to you and the success of your ministry. Each man should know what he can and should do in this matter. Renting is a good idea until you know what your options are for buying. Buying, of course, can be a great investment. Unless you are familiar with the area and situation, be careful about putting roots too deep, too quickly. You should plan to take the time to get settled with your family before jumping into the work of planting the church. Accommodating your family will be time well spent. Your home will be a place where you receive guests, so you want things to be in order.

If at all possible, live near or in the community where you will be starting the new church. Get to know your neighbors, the man at the gas station, the people at the pharmacy, the corner grocery store, etc. Make friends by being friendly.

CHAPTER 5: TEACHING AND PREACHING

Make it a point to meet the city officials. Line up a family doctor. Know where the hospital, the children's school, etc. are located. As you meet new people share your vision, the gospel, and your plans for the beginning of a new congregation. Be sensitive to the Holy Spirit but begin sharing the gospel ASAP. You may be surprised to find some of the new people you meet are not only open to the gospel but have a hunger for God. The Lord did send you there for this purpose, didn't HE?

CHOOSE A NAME FOR THE CHURCH

Give the church a name that identifies it as Baptist. I have a problem with the missionaries that take support from Baptist churches and then do not establish Baptist churches. If you choose a name that identifies the community or area, be careful that the name would still be valid should the church locate a few blocks or streets away. Having a church name will allow you to go ahead with the printing of brochures, the opening of a bank account (savings account), the obtaining of a post-office box, etc.

DECIDE ON A SUITABLE MEETING PLACE

It might be necessary initially to meet in a private home. <u>Avoid using your home if at all possible.</u> You will have little enough privacy as is. Close off the portions of the house that should be private if you do meet in a home. As soon as possible, find a public meeting place. You may find some individuals will not go to the home where you are having services. Old grudges die hard especially in small towns.

There are several possibilities as we have already mentioned. When you rent, it is usually wise to obtain a written contract stating the conditions, privileges, and responsibilities. Check for any permits, approval needed from the local fire

THE BASICS OF CHURCH PLANTING

marshal, insurance certificates of occupancy, and limitations on the number of occupants, ordinances, or anything that might be required or stipulated by law.

WHEN YOU HAVE A PLACE TO MEET, SET A DATE FOR YOUR FIRST SERVICES

When you know you have a place prepared in which to meet, have your literature, church sign, announcements, and all the other items we have mentioned ready so that you can start promoting the first services. Then you can set a date. **Give yourself time to visit daily for four weeks before having the first service.** The idea is to have ample time to let people know what, when, where, why and how. Make it clear that they are invited. Make every effort to have a good crowd present. Have some special folk come in to help if at all possible. Leave no leaf unturned in an effort to have a great beginning. Announce the occasion wherever and however you can (newspaper, radio, TV, flyers, etc.). You will have to work hard. You can rest after the "first service" day is over. It would be better to be over prepared and be disappointed than to announce the first services and not be fully prepared for an overflow crowd. Have some token (an inexpensive bookmark, ribbon, etc.) that they can take home with them as a reminder that they were in the first service of the new church. Nothing will cause people to turn away like feeling that you really didn't expect them to come. Be prepared to record the name and address of every visitor. <u>Expect folk to come and be saved.</u> Be ready to deal with them. Be sharp. Give the impression that you know what you are doing even if you don't. Be prepared to take photos, videos and have a written record of that special service.

<u>FOLLOW UP</u> ON ALL CONTACTS, MAKE PHONE CALLS, VISITS, WRITE LETTERS, AND SEND EMAILS.

Prepare form letters that can serve as the models for

CHAPTER 5: TEACHING AND PREACHING

letters that cover a wide range of contacts including first time visitors, new residents, new converts, and people you contacted through visitation. Most everyone enjoys receiving a letter in the mail. You may find a phone call on Saturday or even Sunday morning is just the personal touch that some folk need to be convinced you care.

In addition to the standard letters we have already mentioned, it might be effective to watch the local newspaper for opportunities to send a congratulatory letter to someone or to possibly send a note of sympathy to someone who is bereaved, etc. There are many small things that a person can do to show love and interest.

NO AMOUNT OF PREPARATION WILL SUFFFICE IF YOU DO NOT BATHE ALL IN PRAYER.

- Pray every day.
- Pray with your family.
- Pray with those who are helping you.
- Pray with the people you meet on visitation.
- Pray for God's direction and blessing in soul winning.
- Pray daily for new converts.
- Pray for deliverance from temptation.
- Pray for protection for you and your family

THE BASICS OF CHURCH PLANTING

- Pray for God's provision
- Pray for labourers.
- Pray about everything.
- Praise Him daily.
- Praise Him for everything.
- Praise Him for who He is as well as what He does.
- Praise His Name.
- Praise the Father.
- Praise the Son.
- Praise the Holy Ghost.
- Magnify Him.
- Make much of Him

CHAPTER SIX

THE PLAN FOR CHURCH PLANTING

The church planter knows it is God's will for him to start a new church. He has found God's will concerning where he is to start the church. He has moved to the area and has made all the preliminary arrangements. Now it is time to get started.

VISITATION AS A TEAM EFFORT

Are you going to have help in the beginning or are you going to work alone?

It is better, in most cases, to have help, especially in the beginning. Help can come from a number of sources. These include:

1. Fellow missionaries

2. Members of the sponsoring church and other nearby churches

3. Bible College students seeking a ministry for the summer

4. A team of people from another church, even from out of state

5. A missions team from a foreign country

It would be great if a fellow missionary could work with you, especially in the first week or two. A missionary from the same area might possibly be able to bring a group of people from his work to assist in door-to-door visitation.

Be flexible. You might be able to schedule your first services at a time when members of a sister church could be present. The very presence of these people in the services will stir interest and attract others.

REMEMBER, PEOPLE ATTRACT PEOPLE

If you are fortunate enough to have some help, be prepared to use that help effectively. Have your brochures and literature ready and available. Obtain maps of the area. Organize the visitation teams so that each house in the area is contacted. The first visits will be for the purpose of making the community aware of the new ministry.

You will need to make sure that the helpers know where to go and what to do. Keep good records so that you will know which homes have received a visit. You may have to instruct the helpers concerning how you expect the visitation to proceed. Advise them of any known dangers or pitfalls.

IDEAS:

Send the helpers in pairs or with three in a group maximum. In certain areas, it is wise that there be a man in each group.

Warn them about entering a home that might put them in a compromising position. If necessary, you can station a man on the corner at the end of the block but in a place where he can observe the visitation teams.

The approach for door-to-door visitation differs for each area (inner city, town, rural).

The initial visits are to make people aware of the new church, but there can be opportunities to witness and win

CHAPTER 6: THE PLAN FOR CHURCH PLANTING

people to Christ. Many good prospects come from these visits. You may have your first converts from them as well.

IT IS ABSOLUTELY NECESSARY TO MAKE NOTE OF ALL PROSPECTS. Get their names and other information so that you can continue to visit them.

YOU MAY MEET:

1. Saved people who are faithful members of a good fundamental church in the area. Don't try to pull them away from their church. Be ethical in the matter.

2. Saved people that are not back in church. Seek to help them get right with the Lord and in church...yours or especially where they are a member. Caution should be applied when dealing with "disgruntled church members." If they are to join with you, past problems should be dealt with so that they don't bring bitterness and other bad attitudes into the new church. <u>Disgruntled church members often become disgruntled, in time, wherever they are.</u> Your ministry probably won't be the exception. They may seem like God's answer to your prayers, at first. It is better to have folk get upset with you before they become members of the church. Once members of the church they will be in a position to have a negative influence on the rest of the congregation.

EVERY PERSON IN YOUR MINISTRY AREA IS A PROSPECT FOR TRUSTING CHRIST AND ATTENDING YOUR CHURCH -- UNTIL PROVEN OTHERWISE.

As you have folk saved and they join with you, encourage them to invite their families, friends, and neighbors. <u>They know far more people than you do</u>, and it is a proven fact that <u>more people visit a church because they are invited by a</u>

friend or family member than because they are invited by the pastor, who may be just a stranger to them.

YOU MAY OBTAIN PROSPECTS THROUGH:

1. Bulk Mailings. The local post office can provide you with information concerning costs, permits, etc.

2. Telephone Surveys. These can be especially effective for reaching the people in apartment complexes or places with limited access.

3. Advertisements in the local newspaper offering a free Bible correspondence course.

4. A Daily Radio Program. Offer the same free Bible study courses.

5. A Community Survey.

6. Get Acquainted Meetings. These meetings are held in a private home. It is preferable not to have them in the pastor's home. The meetings should be informal and relaxed. Three Tuesday nights or Thursday nights before the first public service is a good time to schedule them.

   a. **The first meeting**

   Introductions: You, your families, the helpers, all present. Give information about you and your family. Share your burden. Present the plan of salvation. Ask those interested in being saved to remain after the meeting. Encourage all to come for the second meeting and bring someone with them. Pray. Serve refreshments. Do not ride hobby horses or pick on pet peeves. Major on the Gospel (1 Corinthians 15:1-8); the "death of the Lord for our sins according to the Scripture,

His burial, His resurrection the third day according to the Scripture."

b. The second meeting

Introductions: especially the new people. Explain your burden to establish a new church. Explain that the Bible will be the foundation. Give out literature (brochure, doctrinal statement, explanation of the gospel, etc). Pray. Provide refreshments.

c. The third meeting

Introductions: Give out the literature presenting the new ministry. Explain your goals, burden for souls, etc. Challenge them to trust Christ and get involved in helping start the new church. You need to speak to the issue of commitment to the Lord Jesus Christ. You may want to briefly mention salvation, separation, stewardship, service, etc.

You have a good chance of winning new converts in these meetings. Do follow up. Make disciples. Work with these contacts and converts. Also teach them about soul winning, assisting in some way, etc.

7. Home Bible Studies.

The home Bible Studies can be effective as long as you keep them headed in the right direction. <u>They must not be an end in themselves.</u> They are not to replace the church or its regular services. Their main purpose should be to make new contacts in various locations throughout the community. These prospects should be channeled into the new church. Simple Bible lessons and prayer are the order of the day.

Warning: Supplanters and charismatics love the opportunities afforded in the home Bible studies to sow their seeds of discord and false doctrine.

8. Tent Meetings – Special evangelistic campaigns.

In some areas it is possible to set up a tent and begin anew church by having evangelistic services every night for an extended period of time. This method lends itself better to situations where there is a team of church   planters. Some towns and cities may consider themselves too modern for the old fashion tent meeting. The church planter will have to evaluate and make a judgment call as to whether a tent meeting would be an effective way to begin the new church. Remember to take the climate and weather conditions into consideration

Note:

The great Gospel Light Baptist Church in Walkertown, NC where Bro. Bobby Roberson was pastor began in an extended tent meeting. The "tent meeting" has been used effectively in years past to start and establish churches in Central America.

9. Through a Web-site on the computer.

Detailed preparation for public services

The weeks of visitation and other activities aimed at obtaining good prospects should have resulted in a group of people that God can use to get the church started. You will then be ready to start having regularly scheduled weekly services.

CHAPTER 6: THE PLAN FOR CHURCH PLANTING

Note:

The group of people that you start with may not be with you after six months. Some will leave you when they see what is going on and come face to face with the commitment that is required. **Don't faint.** God will send new folk to you to replace them.

MAKE A CHECKLIST.

- ☑ Have you chosen a name?
- ☑ Have you obtained a mailing address and checking account for the church?
- ☑ Have you acquired (rent, etc.) an adequate place to meet?
- ☑ Do you have your church signs in place?
- ☑ Do you have your church brochure ready?
- ☑ Have you had the three "get acquainted" meetings?
- ☑ Are you prepared for visitors (brochures, visitor's cards, etc.)?
- ☑ Have you made every effort to announce to the community what you are doing?
- ☑ Have you spent the necessary time in door-to-door visitation?
- ☑ Are you praying without ceasing?

We have covered briefly the things that need to be in place before you start regular services. **The "keys" will be visitation for soul winning purposes and an effort to saturate your area with announcements and invitations.**

Again, any special help that you can get in the days leading up to and including the first public services will be invaluable. If you don't have any help, don't be discouraged. God knows where you are and He is with you. We have had both situations. One time, we started with just our family (me, my wife, and our baby girl) and one local man. On other occasions, we have had a team and several local people to get started.

GIVE THOUGHT TO:

1. The meeting place (chairs, pulpit, piano, classrooms, nursery and supplies, restrooms, water fountain, literature, hymnals, Bibles, offering plates, a/c, or heat, lighting, sound equipment, etc.

2. Visitor cards, offering envelopes, decision cards.

3. Workers. If you are alone, you will have to handle everything yourself with the help of your family. If you have people that you can train to help with the nursery, ushering, song leading, playing the instruments, personal work at the altar or other duties, you will be blessed.

4. Order of service. Be punctual. Have good music or no music. In many cases it is not necessary to have a hymnal. You may copy just the words or project them on a screen using an overhead projector. Make a brief explanation of why you are starting the new church. Explain <u>briefly</u> each aspect of the service. This may be new to your folk. Preach a brief (30 min. max.) gospel message. It is better to leave folk with a desire for more than to wear them out by giving them everything you know in one message. Give an invitation. Share with the congregation any responses. Invite all to return for the next service. Encourage them to bring someone. **Pray.**

Evaluate the service, the results, the responses, etc.

Make adjustments.

A strong church must have:

1. **<u>Spiritual</u> growth and stability.**

    You want to see people saved but there should also be spiritual growth and progress in their lives.

2. **<u>Numerical</u> growth and stability.**

    Of course it is more exciting to have numbers of people saved as opposed to a few. The quantity of fruit you reap will most likely be directly related to the amount of sowing you do... with some exceptions. Some fields are very difficult and there may be few visible results from all of your sowing. Be faithful.

3. **<u>Financial</u> growth and stability.**

    If you are able to win converts and disciple them, you should see them begin to give to the Lord. Teach them to tithe and give offerings, by faith, unto the Lord.

    WORK TOWARD THESE GOALS.

CHAPTER SEVEN
REPETITION AIDS IN LEARNING

Building the Church on the Field

This seems like a good time to remind you of the Scriptural pattern of **evangelism, edification or instruction and entrusting...**

Scriptures to consider:

1. Matthew 28:19-20

*"**Go** ye therefore, and **teach all nations**, baptizing them in the name of the Father, and of the Son, and of the Holy Ghost: **Teaching them to observe all things whatsoever I have commanded you:** and, lo, I am with you always, even unto the end of the world."*

2. Ephesians 4:11-16

"And He gave some, apostles; and some, prophets; and some, evangelists; and some, pastors and teachers; For the perfecting of the saints, for the work of the ministry, for the edifying of the body of Christ: Till we all come in the unity of the faith, and of the knowledge of the Son of God, unto a perfect man, unto the measure of the stature of the fullness of Christ: That we henceforth be no more children, tossed to and fro, and carried about with every wind of doctrine, by the sleight of men, and cunning craftiness, whereby they lie in wait to deceive; But speaking

CHAPTER 7: REPETITION AIDS IN LEARNING

the truth in love, may grow up in Him in all things, which is the head, even Christ; From whom the whole body fitly joined together and compacted by that which every joint supplieth, according to the effectual working in the measure of every part, maketh increase of the body unto the edifying of itself in love."

3. Acts 14:21-23

*"And when they had **preached the gospel to that city**, and **had taught many**, they returned again to Lystra, and to Iconium, and Antioch, **confirming the souls** of **the disciples**, and **exhorting them** to continue in the faith, and that we must through much tribulation enter into the kingdom of God. And when **they had ordained them elders in every church**, and **had prayed with fasting**, **they commended them to the Lord**, on whom they believed."*

4. Acts 20:28, 32

"Take heed therefore unto yourselves, and to all the flock, over the which the Holy Ghost hath made you overseers, to feed the church of God, which He hath purchased with his own blood."

*"And now, brethren, **I commend you to God, and to the word** of his grace, which is able **to build you up**, and give you an inheritance among all them which are **sanctified.**"*

5. 2 Timothy 2:2; 3:10

*"And the things that thou hast heard of me among many witnesses, the same **commit thou to**

faithful men, who shall be able to teach others also."

"But thou hast fully known my doctrine, manner of life, purpose, faith, longsuffering, charity, patience, persecutions, afflictions..."

5. Matthew 16:18

*"And I say unto thee, That thou art Peter, and upon this rock **I will build my church**; and the gates of hell shall not prevail against it."*

Considerations:

A. Every Christian and every Bible believing congregation should be involved in missions... church planting. The Great Commission given by the Lord Jesus Christ is only partially fulfilled if evangelism is our only objective.

B. Where it is possible and practical new churches should be planted by existing local churches. (Churches planting churches)

C. On some fields there are no fundamental Bible believing churches present to help directly in the effort of starting and establishing new churches. In these cases the pioneer missionary church planter would have to begin the new church as a mission or extension of his sending church. **Though God uses mission agencies to assist the local church and the missionary, the local congregation should remain at the center of all missionary activity.**

D. There is a difference between *starting* and *establishing* a new church. It may only require a few days or weeks to sow the seeds (to plant) for the

CHAPTER 7: REPETITION AIDS IN LEARNING

beginning of a new church but to establish the congregation into an indigenous church will most likely require several years.

E. The local church has three ministries:

1. The ministry to the **lost**... **evangelism**

2. The ministry to the **saved**... **edification**, instruction, exhortation, etc.

3. The ministry to **God**... **exaltation**, worship, service, etc.

F. To establish a truly indigenous church on the field should be the goal.

G. The **church planter should "partner with God.**

*"For **we are labourers together with God**: ye are God's husbandry, ye are God's building."* (I Corinthians 3:9)

These are not just idle words. This must be a reality in the life of the church planter. We must work in partnership with the Lord.

KEY NUMBER ONE:
A PERSONAL DAILY WALK with the Lord

A personal daily walk with the Lord defined by **prayer, occasional fasting and devotional study of the Bible** is absolutely necessary if we are to accomplish the task. Remember we are in a spiritual battle and we are storming the "gates of hell" as we move into a new area to win souls and establish Christ's church.

Ephesians 6:12-13.

"For we wrestle not against flesh and blood, but against principalities, against powers, against the rulers of the darkness of this world, against spiritual wickedness in high places. Wherefore take unto you the whole armour of God..."

To fail in this area will bring spiritual weakness and probable failure.

We should partner with the Lord Jesus Christ and the Holy Ghost because:

1. Jesus promised to "build His church." Matthew 16:18

2. Jesus purchased the church. Acts 20:28

3. Jesus provides "redemption." Titus 2:14

4. Jesus and His finished work are the message. 1 Corinthians 14:1-4

5. Jesus has sent the Person of the Holy Ghost to give power. Acts 1:8; John 16:7-11

    The Holy Spirit is here in Jesus place and as a divine person convicts sinners and draws them to the Lord.

John 15:5

"I am the vine, ye are the branches: He that abideth in me, and I in him, the same bringeth forth much fruit: for <u>without me ye can do nothing.</u>"

Psalm 127:1

"*Except the LORD build the house*, *they labor in vain that build it*":
WE MUST MAINTAIN THE RIGHT RELATIONSHIP WITH THE LORD. WE DESPERATELY NEED HIS PRESENCE AND POWER AND BLESSING UPON THE CHURCH PLANTING MINISTRY.

We can have all the right methods and programs but it comes down to being filled with the Holy Spirit and being blessed by HIM. The Lord Jesus Christ has worked in the church planter's life to save and call into the ministry. He has provided all that is necessary to accomplish the task. He is more interested and concerned about the winning of the lost and the establishment of new churches than we can ever be. It only makes sense to work in unity and harmony with HIM.

Remember that what I say comes from my experiences as a church planter in towns and cities in Central America. The Scripture and biblical methods remain constant but there must be some adjusts for differences of culture, language, social structure, etc.

The church planter must be a:

1. Soul winner

2. Teacher... a maker of disciples

3. Mentor... one who trains leaders for the new church.

KEY NUMBER TWO: EVANGELISM

Assuming that all is in order for us to take the first steps for planting a new church we begin with **EVANGELISM**.

Evangelism should be **a way of life** for the church planter.

Every person in the town or city where the church planter is serving should be seen as **a prospect** for salvation, baptism, and membership in the new church... until proven otherwise.

Each day should begin with **prayer** and possibly as expressed in the little chorus...

> Lord lay some soul upon my heart
>
> and love that soul through me
>
> and may I humbly do my part
>
> to win that soul to thee.

One writer has stated that the first consideration is **CONTACTS**. Whether called contacts, prospects or potential believers and members of the new church is not as important as the fact that the church planter should be availing himself of every opportunity to share the good news of the gospel.

The Apostle Paul sets the example for us in Acts 16:12. As soon as he and the others of the missionary team arrived in Philippi they went to the place where they might find

CHAPTER 7: REPETITION AIDS IN LEARNING

prospects... "The river side, where prayer was wont to be made".

The church planter need not wait for some "formal" program of visitation to start winning souls. Start the very first day with the contacts you make in the course of getting your family settled, renting a house, buying groceries, gasoline, arranging for mail delivery, finding a family doctor, ordering the newspaper, having the phone installed, etc, etc,

Practicing **personal evangelism as a way of life** means you will always have your soul winner's New Testament and gospel tracts available. Because you have prayed for souls today you will be sensitive to the direction of the Holy Ghost. You will look for opportunities and open doors. You will be gracious and compassionate even in the face of closed doors leaving a good testimony, hoping for them to open another day.

The church planter who lives in the town targeted by he and his family can benefit greatly from having a good testimony before everyone he meets. Share Christ, the gospel, your reason for being there. Be confident but not obnoxious. Walk with God. Don't be a recluse, a hermit, a stranger. Make friends... even with those that you cannot win right away. Be human. Be real. Reflect Christ's image.

ACTS 16:10

"And after he had seen the vision, immediately we endeavored to go into Macedonia, assuredly gathering that the Lord had called us for to <u>preach the gospel</u> unto them."

ACTS 14:21

"And when they had <u>preached the gospel</u> to that city..."

The emphasis in these verses is on the "preaching of the gospel." This speaks to us of the apostles efforts to evangelize the people of that city. By the way, the fact that it says, "...to that city" points out that they were concerned that the whole city have the opportunity to hear the good news of Christ.

When one preaches the "gospel" he is presenting the good news of **1 Corinthians 15:1-4**, the **"death of Christ for our sins according to the Scripture, His burial and His resurrection according to the Scripture.** This is the message needed for salvation.

Soulwinning……..Considerations:
A. Do personal soul winning.

> **1. Time:** The church planter should plan on doing, as a minimum 20-30 hours a week of personal soul winning to get started. As time goes along your schedule will change, but to get started spend many hours knocking on doors. It is always best to go as a couple if possible. Having your wife along will open doors and allow you to go where you should not go alone. It will help build a testimony as a family man.
>
> **2. Target:** It is not wrong to target a particular group of people or section of town to get started. Most missionaries target poor areas. This is possibly because they are not as intimidated by

these folk or possibly because many of the poor are more open to strangers and new ideas. Christ died for the middle and upper classes too. Go where God leads you.

3. **Follow-up:** Keep good records of visits made, results, opportunities, etc. This will necessitate having visitation cards, tracts, invitations to the church, Gospels of John and Romans, etc. If all else fails at least have a note pad in which to write down names and addresses. This is your life. Be sharp. Souls hang in the balance.

4. **First Impressions:** Remember the people's first impression may be their last. Dress properly. If wearing a suit is impractical for door to door or hut to hut visitation, dress accordingly. If a white shirt and tie identify you with the members of a false cult, wear something else when out in the street.

B. Evangelism: Special Activities

1. Churches planting churches

If you are blessed to have a local church close enough to be the sponsoring church then there are many activities that can be planned to facilitate the establishment of a new church.

Select a number of mature members that can do soul winning and serve in other capacities from the mother church, those who are representatives of what a Christian should be. Take them to the target area for **door to door visitation.** They can do a survey, soul winning and leave information about the new church. This multiplies the number of contacts that can be made and, hopefully the number of souls won initially. They should record the names, ages, and addresses of prospects and converts. As the group goes from week to week hopefully a number of people will have been converted.

When there are new converts attention should be given immediately to the **need of discipleship.** Those having won new converts should schedule a time with them when they can begin the discipleship process. There are discipleship courses available in many languages (Striving Together Publications, The Old Paths Publications, Inc., etc.) so it should not be necessary for you to take your valuable time as a soul winner and maker of disciples to translate and print new materials. There is no need to re-invent the wheel.

There may be place for the members of the sponsoring church to help with:

1. Open air services... showing a gospel film, skits, drama, etc.

2. Evangelistic campaigns in public buildings (community centers, convention centers, sports facilities, etc.) using the members of the sponsoring church as personal workers.

3. Medical crusades in support of the church-planting efforts..

4. Other activities (suppers, lady's or men's breakfasts, camps, seminars, vacation Bible schools, retreats or advances, etc.

Once there are some new converts and they are being discipled the next step is to work toward "congregating them in one central location." The members of the mother church will be a benefit when singing hymns, having Sunday School (S.S.) classes of various ages... even if it is Tuesday night or Thursday evening. The church will not be organized in a moment or a day. It is a matter of doing evangelism, discipleship and moving toward formality of service, worship, etc. Do not wait long before having baptisms.

Encourage the new converts to attend and invite their families and friends. **Get them involved.** A part of their discipleship training should cover how to win souls. The church planter will lose his soul-winning team when the members of the mother church leave, so he needs to work toward building a new team... those of his new congregation.

Start the new church through EVANGELISM.

KEY NUMBER THREE:
Edification, or Instruction

Acts 14:21 "And when they had preached the gospel to that city, and had taught many..."

From the moment the church planter wins a soul to Christ he needs to begin the process of instructing, edifying, or teaching the new convert. Matthew 28:20

Reach the new converts, and then begin to teach them

Notice Hebrews 5:11-6:12. To teach the new converts the "first principles of the oracles of God is to lay a foundation on which they can build their spiritual lives. A number of well taught converts will be necessary to make up the foundation or charter group of the new church. In Hebrews 5:11-12 the writer points out the problem that arises when the work of making disciples is left undone or done carelessly. It is not enough to simply preach doctrine from the pulpit or even to go over it in Sunday School. The new convert needs one-on-one attention, under most circumstances.

By communicating the doctrines of the Bible to the new convert on a one-on-one basis the church planter can communicate his biblical convictions and his heart. The one being discipled can ask questions that might not be asked in a group setting. He can express his doubts, confusion, and even rejection of certain truths, allowing the church planter to know better the people with which he is working and expects to establish a church.

<u>It would be a grave mistake to accept people as charter members of a new church who do not hold to the doctrinal position of the church.</u> Though all preaching should be Scriptural and replete with Bible doctrine it should be remembered that the pulpit is not the place to deal with the sins or specific needs of individuals. Christ's ministry was both public and private. He used the times when alone with His disciples to instruct them and bring them along as His disciples.

BE A TEACHER

The Lord, according to Ephesians 4:11-16, gave the evangelist (evangelist and gospel have the same Greek root,

CHAPTER 7: REPETITION AIDS IN LEARNING

[evvangelion] "good news") but He also gave the pastors and teachers.

According to the progression seen in these verses the person won to Christ through the "work of the evangelist" is, through the ministry of the pastors and teachers, to be:

A. **"Perfected."** Compare Hebrews 6:1 and Matthew 5:48. The word "perfected" implies full development, growth into maturity of godliness, not sinless perfection. The idea is of the "maturing" of the believer through the process of instruction and application of the Scripture. The one who is "making a disciple" cooperates with the Holy Spirit to give to the new convert the foundation or biblical basis for growth in the Lord.

B. The new convert is instructed in the Word so that he can become involved in the **"work of the ministry"** for the purpose of edifying or building up the body of Christ;

    1.) In number as a soul winner... **quantity**

    2.) In Christian character as a true disciple of Christ... **quality**

C. The ministry of edification is so that there might be a nucleus of maturing believers;

    1.) United –"unity of the faith," sound doctrine being the standard or basis for unity.

    2.) Unity in the knowledge of the Son of God...

    To know Him, not just about Him.

3.) **"A perfect man"** – the body of Christ.

4.) **"Unto the measure... of Christ".** The Lord is the standard. The church members are to be conformed to His image.

5.) **"No more children**" *tossed to and fro, and carried about with every wind of doctrine..."*

"by the sleight of men, and cunning craftiness, whereby they lie in wait to deceive; but speaking the truth in love, may grow up into him in all things, which is the head, even Christ; From whom the whole body fitly joined together and compacted by that which every joint supplieth, according to the effectual working in the measure of every part, maketh increase of the body unto the edifying of itself in love." (Eph 4:14-16)

The relationship developed between the disciple and the maker of disciples will be a foundation, also, for the **fourth key** for building a church on the field... **the training of leaders.**

KEY NUMBER FOUR:
Training Leaders

As you, live among and minister to your people use every opportunity to share your love for Christ, for His Church and share your knowledge of His Word, your passion for His will, and your vision of a Christ-honoring local church in the area. They will learn much from your teaching but they will also learn from association with you, from seeing your life, from being with you.

2 Timothy 2:2

"And the things that thou hast heard of me among many witnesses, **<u>the same commit thou to faithful men, who shall be able to teach others also.</u>***"*

1. Teach your people what they should know biblically and then give them opportunities to use and teach what they have learned.

2. Allow them to make mistakes. You and I make our share.

3. Do not scold them in public. Treat them as you would want to be treated. Correct them in private with the idea of building them up not tearing them down.

4. Respect them and they will be more likely to respect you.

5. Trust them and they will more readily trust you.

6. It is a wise man that counsels himself with others. The nationals on a foreign field or in a cross-cultural setting may very well know some things you ignore. With special care have a confidant (keep in mind that your wife should be your most trusted friend and confidant) who can help you with things you may not recognize, language errors, oversights, etc. Be careful that what you share will edify and not cause others to stumble. The Bible does call a man that "tells all he knows" a fool.

7. Teach them how to make wise decisions by including them in the decision making process in matters having to do with the church.

8. Trust the Holy Spirit to do in them what He has done in you – and more.

9. Seek their success and you will enjoy and share their success. Their success will make you a success.

10. Make the new church theirs.

11. Teach them to give.

12. Teach them to live by faith, to look to the Lord... not you, the mission agency or the churches in the USA.

13. Do not teach them they are too poor to give in support of the local ministry, missionaries or to build their own temple.

14. Train your people to do personal work, to be soul winners.

15. Train them to disciple others.

16. Train them to train others.

17. Train them to lead the services, the singing, etc.

18. Teach them to maintain order and sound doctrine.

19. Train them in correct church discipline.

20. Train them in the selection of leaders, deacons, pastors, teachers, nursery workers, singers, etc.

CHAPTER 7: REPETITION AIDS IN LEARNING

Note:

It may seem cold and business like but there is nothing wrong with letting people know up front that you are looking for people who will be serious about faithfully serving the Lord and honoring His Word.

In order to train the people you will need to have materials on hand that help you present this type of training in an orderly fashion. Be biblical in your teaching. Do not say, "It is this way because I say so." Teach Bible principles.

The Bible does not speak directly to all the issues people face. This is why it is also important to reach "principles" that can be used to guide us when there is no direct word given concerning a matter. For example the Bible does not say, "Thou shalt not smoke." The Bible does say we are not to defile or do damage to our physical body because it is the "temple of the Holy Spirit." Smoking harms the body. The conclusion is that we should not smoke or use tobacco.

People need to know why they believe what they believe and why things are done the way they are.

Be careful about building permanent scaffolding. The church must stand on its own. Let it be indigenous or autonomous.

If the church planter does his job following this biblical pattern (Acts 14:21-23) he will be able to move on to start another new church... he will have worked himself out of a job in this church. He can move on, "having commended the new church to the Lord on whom they believed. Of course if the missionary plans to establish a central church out of which many more churches can be established in partnership with the national leaders God has raised up, then he will have a good foundation on which to build his continuing ministry. It is a real joy (Phil 4:1-2) when one's disciples excel and surpass him in the knowledge of God, in commitment to HIS will and in his daily walk with God.

It probably is evident to some that nothing has been said about building a building. Most nationals are capable of providing a building for themselves if given the opportunity. From experience I found that **it is far more important to build the church than to build a building.** One of the strongest churches we started and established met in a rented building until after we left the field. Under national leaders lead by Pastor Rene Claros they purchased land and built a building and they did this during 12 years of revolution.

To avoid the questionable practice of some missionaries who move right into a "building project dependent on foreign funds" once they have 20-30 people in attendance, one can do one of several things.

➢ Start a "building fund" account from the very beginning.

➢ Use the present facility to the maximum.

- This may mean remodeling (with the owner's permission of course) or building a temporary tabernacle (upright posts or columns and a roof).

- Using a large tent has often served the purpose.

- It may mean having double services – an early service for part of the congregation and a later service for the remainder.

- It might mean renting another house or facility or a vacant lot, next door.

CHAPTER 7: REPETITION AIDS IN LEARNING

The simple fact is that missionaries often feel they have to raise foreign funds and dedicate the major portion of their time and energies in the construction of a building. They neglect the necessary soul winning and discipleship of new converts to do this. If foreign churches and individuals do not respond with donations as expected, the missionary may become discouraged and develop a negative attitude.

I will admit that there are times when a missionary is wise to seek to purchase a key piece of property in a good location in order to get a better price. This decision should only be made after consulting with the missionary's sending pastor and where a mission agency is involved, with the Field Director and even other missionaries on the field. Every effort should be made to teach the new congregation that it is their responsibility to cover the amount the missionary and other churches may invest in this purchase.

There are missionaries serving in very difficult places like New York City or Tokyo, Japan where it will most likely be nigh impossible for them to ever purchase a piece of property or a building. In spite of this a local church can be established.

Win souls. Make disciples. Build the Church!

Lay a firm foundation by teaching the biblical truths upon which Christianity stands.

CHAPTER EIGHT

THE ORGANIZATION OF THE LOCAL CHURCH

Once the new church is functioning and holding regular weekly services or meetings and there have been several adults saved and discipled, it is time to plan for the formal organization of the church. An in-depth teaching in the following areas should precede the organization of the church:

1. Fundamental or basic Bible doctrine (Hebrews 5:11-6:2). A complete study of the church's Statement of Faith.

2. Historical Baptist distinctives. Biblical (Baptist) practice, polity, etc.

3. A complete and thorough study of the local New Testament church – The church, its role in world evangelization, its ministry, organization, officials, ordinances, etc.

4. The responsibilities, privileges, and opportunities for service of the individual members.

It is extremely important that the group of believers with which you plan to organize the church understand and accept the truths, principles, and responsibilities that are presented in the various documents of the church. A church planter that does not see the importance of this matter will build a "house of straw." **Fellowship and unity should be based on common Bible doctrine.**

One church planter I know went to the extreme of accepting people that he suspected of being unsaved as members in his new church thinking that he would be able to win them to the Lord. He now sees the mistake he made by swinging the doors of church membership open to "whosoever wants to be a charter member."

The following documents need to be prepared before the organization of the church. We have suggested that it is best to place these in the hands of the new members at the very beginning.

The Charter of the Church

This is a formal statement in which the group, comprising the membership of the new congregation, declares itself to be an autonomous church with Christ granted authority to exercise all the rights and responsibilities of a New Testament Church. The wording of the "Charter" may provide for the adoption of other church documents, or they may be adopted separately.

The Church Constitution

The constitution defines the administrative procedures by which the church functions, the rules, the regulations, and the requirements for membership and leadership. The constitution of the church, which is based on the principles found in the New Testament, is the guiding document by which the church is governed.

The Doctrinal Statement

The beliefs of the church are set forth in this document. The church's position on all major doctrines should be set forth in clear and detailed fashion. There can also be provision for a statement of the church's position in such matters as the ecumenical movement, neo-orthodoxy, neo-evangelism, the charismatic movement, modernistic theology, ecclesiastical separation, modern versions of the Bible and modern trends.

There are examples of these documents included in this book. You should also be able to obtain copies from your home church or missions agency.

CHAPTER 8: THE ORGANIZATION OF THE LOCAL CHURCH

CHARTER

Of the

(Name of church)

(City, state)

On this   day of   we the undersigned, having received Jesus Christ as our personal Saviour and being baptized by immersion in obedience to His command, do hereby constitute ourselves to be an independent Baptist church patterned after the New Testament example.

Moreover, this church through the authority invested in it by Jesus Christ shall have the right to administer the ordinances of believer's baptism by immersion and the Lord's Supper and shall seek the salvation of the lost through the proclamation of the Gospel while encouraging one another in Christian love.

Furthermore, this church shall be governed by the will of God as revealed in the Holy Scriptures and in accordance with the covenant, the constitution, and the articles of faith, which we do hereby adopt by the affixing of our signatures to this document.

Sample Document #1

CHURCH COVENANT

Having been led by the Holy Spirit of God to receive the Lord Jesus Christ as my personal Savior, and having been baptized by immersion in obedience to His Word, I enter into covenant with the members of the local congregation. I promise by the aid of the Holy Spirit to:

Honor Jesus Christ through my efforts to advance His cause: by seeking the salvation of my relatives and acquaintances: by having family and personal devotions: and by training my children according to the Word of God.

Help this church by promoting its spirituality, program, and prosperity and by attending its services regularly.

Walk in Christian love by avoiding gossip, slander, and anger; by praying for the members of this church and helping them in sickness or distress; by cultivation of Christian empathy and courtesy; and by being sincere and without offense.

Walk wisely by being honest and exemplary in my conduct; by dressing modestly and appropriately; and by abstaining from anything that would be a detriment to my testimony for Christ. Furthermore, I promise to abstain from the use of alcoholic beverages and/or drugs for non-medicinal purposes.

If I move from this area, I will unite as soon as possible with another Bible-believing, fundamental Baptist church in

CHAPTER 8: THE ORGANIZATION OF THE LOCAL CHURCH

which I can carry out the principles of the Word of God and the spirit of this covenant.

Sample Document #2

MEMBERSHIP COVENANT

Having been brought together providentially by our common relationship to Jesus Christ as our Savior, and having a mutual desire to serve Him faithfully as our Lord, we do now both solemnly and joyfully enter into covenant with one another as a body of baptized believers comprising a New Testament local church.

WE PURPOSE THEREFORE to live daily by the strength and guidance of God's Holy Spirit; to search the Scriptures regularly and faithfully for direction in personal, family and church life; to seek the salvation of souls for whom Christ died; to strive heartily for the building up of this Body of Christ in faith, hope and love; and to function within the Body according to the gift(s) given each one for its benefit.

WE FURTHER PURPOSE to put away from us progressively the patterns of thought, word and deed of the "old life," putting in its place the patterns of the "Christ-life"; to do all things to the glory of God and in the name of the Lord Jesus; to exercise our Christian liberty in such a way as not to grieve, offend or cause our brother to stumble; and to recognize the Bible as the final Authority in all relationships with one another.

TO THESE ENDS WE PURPOSE to consider the local church an essential part of our lives; to pray for, encourage, and submit to the rightful authority of its leadership; to attend its meetings when not providentially hindered; to support financially its ministry as God enables and directs; to guard its public testimony; and in any way possible to further its goals of reaching the lost and teaching the believer.

CHAPTER 8: THE ORGANIZATION OF THE LOCAL CHURCH

THIS COVENANT WE MAKE GLADLY, in humble dependence upon the Spirit of God for the power to carry out its provisions.

Sample Document #3

DOCTRINAL STATEMENT

1. We believe in the Scriptures of the Old and New Testaments as verbally inspired of God and inerrant, and that they are of supreme and final authority in faith and life. That the King James Version of the Bible is God's preserved Word for English speaking peoples.(2 Timothy 3:16,17; 2 Peter 1:19-21)

2. We believe in one God, eternally existing in three persons: Father, Son, and Holy Spirit. (Exodus 20:2,3; Matthew 28:19; 1 Corinthians 8:6)

3. We believe in God's direct creation of the universe, without the use of pre-existent material, and apart from any process of evolution whatever, according to the Genesis account. (Genesis 1:1-31; Exodus 20:11; Colossians 1:16,17; Hebrews 11:3)

4. We believe that Jesus Christ was begotten by the Holy Spirit and born of Mary, a virgin, and is true God and true man. (Isaiah 7:14; Luke 1:35; Galatians 4:4)

5. We believe that the Lord Jesus Christ died for our sins according to the Scriptures as a representative and substitutionary sacrifice, and that all who believe in Him are justified on the grounds of His shed blood. (Isaiah 53:4-11; Acts 13:38,39; Romans 3:24,25; 4:5, 5:1,8,9, 6:23; 2 Corinthians 5:19-21)

6. We believe in the resurrection of the crucified body of our Lord, in His ascension into heaven, and in His present life there as High Priest and Advocate. (Matthew 28:1-7; Acts 1:8-11; 1 Corinthians 15:4-9; Hebrews 4:14-16)

7. We believe that the Holy Spirit baptizes, seals, and indwells every believer at the moment of salvation and that the Holy Spirit empowers every believer for holy living. We believe that the Holy Spirit today bestows service gifts upon believers and that the sign gifts were restricted to the apostolic period. (Ephesians 1:13, 4:11-12, 5:18; Romans 8:9, 12:6-8; 1 Corinthians 12:13; Hebrews 2:3,4; I Corinthians 13:8-13; Ephesians 2:20)

CHAPTER 8: THE ORGANIZATION OF THE LOCAL CHURCH

8. We believe that man was created in the image of God; that he sinned and thereby incurred not only physical death but also that spiritual death which is separation from God; that all human beings are born with a sinful nature and are sinners in thought, word, and deed. (Genesis 1:26,27, 3:1-6; Romans 5:12, 19, 3:10-13; Titus 1:15,16)

9. We believe that all that receive by faith the Lord Jesus Christ are born again of the Holy Spirit and thereby become children of God. (John 1:12,13, 3:3-16; Acts 16:31; Ephesians 2:8,9)

10. We believe in the "Eternal Security" of the believer, that it is impossible for one born into the family of God ever to be lost. (John 6:39,49, 10:28,29; Romans 8:35-39; Jude 1)

11. We believe in "that blessed hope": the personal, premillennial, pretribulational, and imminent return of our Lord and Savior Jesus Christ, when the Church will be "gathered together unto Him." (John 14:1-3; 1 Thessalonians 4:13-18; 1 Corinthians 15:51-58; 2 Thessalonians 2:1-13)

12. We believe in the literal fulfillment of the prophecies and promises of the Scriptures, which foretell and assure the future regeneration and restoration of Israel as a nation. (Genesis 13:14-17; Jeremiah 16:14,15, 30:6-11; Romans 11)

13. We believe in the bodily resurrection of the just and the unjust, the everlasting blessedness of the saved, and the everlasting punishment of the lost. (Matthew 25:31-46; Luke 16:19-31; 1 Thessalonians 4:13-18; Revelation 21:1-8)

14. We believe that a local New Testament Baptist Church is an organized body of believers immersed upon a credible confession of faith in Jesus Christ, having two offices (pastors and deacon), congregational in polity, autonomous in nature, and banded together for work, worship, the observance of the ordinances and the worldwide proclamation of the gospel. We further believe in the church, which is Christ's body, the spiritual organism consisting of all born-again believers of the New Testament dispensation. (Matthew 28:18-20; Acts 2:41,42; 1 Corinthians 12:13; Ephesians 1:22,23; 1 Timothy 3; I Peter 5:1-3)

15. We believe that the Scriptural ordinances of the church are Baptism and the Lord's Supper and are to be administered by the local church; that Baptism, by immersion, should be administered to believers only as a

symbol of their belief in the death, burial and resurrection of our Lord and Savior Jesus Christ and as a testimony to the world of that belief and of their death, burial and resurrection with Him; and that the Lord's Supper should be partaken of by baptized believers to show forth His death, "till He come." (Matthew 28:18-20; Acts 2:41-47, 8:26-39; 1 Corinthians 11:23-28; Colossians 2:12)

Sample Document #4

ARTICLES OF INCORPORATION

Of the

(Name) Baptist Church of (City), (State)

Article I

We the undersigned do hereby associate ourselves together for the purpose of forming a religious, non-profit corporation, in accordance with Chapter ____ of the State Statutes, and we do hereby adopt the following Articles of Incorporation:

Article II

The name of this corporation, which is a congregation of believers, shall be known as (name of the church) and shall be located at (complete address).

The corporation is and shall be charitable in its nature. The objective of the corporation shall be to minister the Gospel of Jesus Christ for all purposes required in or consistent with the Bible, including but not limited to the purpose of:

1. Evangelizing the lost through personal soul-winning, visitation, and preaching of the Word of God;

2. Edifying believers through the systematic teaching of the Bible;

3. Establishing fundamental Baptist churches around the world through an energetic missions program;

4. Educating our adults and their children in a manner consistent with the requirements of the

Holy Scriptures, both in Sunday and weekday schools of Christian education.

Article III

This church shall be an independent, autonomous Baptist church subject only to Jesus Christ, its Head. It shall have the authority to conduct itself as a Baptist church in accordance with the Word of God as interpreted by the Covenant, Constitution and Articles of Faith adopted by this church.

This church has the right to cooperate and associate with other fundamental Baptist groups on a voluntary basis, but shall not be subject to any control by such groups. This church shall not associate nor cooperate with any person or group who is a part of, or cooperates with liberalism, neo-evangelicalism, the charismatic movement, secret societies, or cults. It has the right to disassociate from any group with which it may have become affiliated.

Article IV

The government of this church shall be vested in its membership. Membership in this church shall be open to all those who:

1) Profess to be born again through faith in Jesus Christ alone;

2) Have been baptized by immersion under the authority of a Baptist church, following their profession of faith;

3) Are in agreement with the Covenant, Constitution, and Articles of Faith of this church.

Membership shall not be denied to any person on the basis of race, color, sex, or social status.

The presence of seventy-five percent of the voting members shall constitute a quorum. Active members in good standing who are sixteen years of age and older shall be eligible

CHAPTER 8: THE ORGANIZATION OF THE LOCAL CHURCH

to vote, except in those matters for which the law of this State requires the minimum age to be higher.

The pastor and deacons shall serve as the trustees (directors) of this corporation.

Article V

This church shall have the right to own, buy, or sell tangible properties, both real and personal, in its own name and through properly elected officers, when so authorized by vote of this church.

No part of the incomes of this corporation shall accrue to the benefit of, or be distributable to any officers, trustee, or member of this corporation or to any other private person; provided however, that the corporation shall be authorized and empowered to pay reasonable compensation for services rendered and expenses incurred in furtherance of the purposes for the corporation.

Notwithstanding any other provision of these Articles, the corporation shall not carry on any other activities not permitted to be carried on by a corporation exempt from Federal income tax under Section 501 (3) C of the Internal Revenue Code of 1954 or corresponding sections of any prior or future Internal Revenue Code or federal, state or local government for exclusive public purpose.

Article VI

In the event of the dissolution of the church, all of its debts shall be paid in full. None of its remaining assets or holdings shall be divided among the members or other individuals, but shall be irrevocably designated by corporate vote of this church prior to dissolution to non-profit fundamental Baptist organizations which are in agreement with the Articles of Faith adopted by this church and in conformity with the requirements of the United States Internal Revenue Service Code of 1954 (Section 501 (3) C and the laws of this state.

IN WITNESS WHEREOF, we, the undersigned subscribers, have hereunto set our hands and seal. This _____ day of _____ 20 ____.

   (Signatures)   (Residence)

_____

_____

_____

_____

_____

_____

State of _____ County of _____

BEFORE ME, the undersigned authority personally appeared (names of the above signatories) known to me to be the subscribers to the foregoing Articles of Incorporation of (<u>name of the church</u>) and they acknowledge to me that they intend in good faith to carry out the purposes and objects set forth in the foregoing Articles of Incorporation.

WITNESS, my hand and official seal at (address where signing occurs), this _____ day of _____. 20_____.

_____

(Signature of notary public)

SAMPLE CONSTITUTION

_____ BAPTIST CHURCH

Of ___City and State_____

PREAMBLE

We, the members of _____BAPTIST CHURCH, in orderly manner do hereby establish the following principles by which we mutually agree to be governed in the affairs of our church.

ARTICLE I – NAME

The name of this organization as incorporated under the laws of _____, shall be _____BAPTIST CHURCH OF _____, _____.

ARTICLE II – PURPOSE

The purpose of this local church shall be to:

(1) To carry out the great commission of Christ, as given in Matthew 2:19-20.

(2) The administration of the ordinances of the New Testament, baptism and the Lord's Supper.

(3) To edify the saints of God through the preaching and teaching of the Word of God as set forth in the Articles of Faith of this church.

(4) Means of Promoting the Purposes: In order to fulfill these purposes, this church shall engage in activities and conduct ministries which may include, but are not limited to, worship services, evangelistic services, prayer meetings, youth activities, radio and television programs, a day school, a Sunday school, a bus ministry, missionary activities, nursing homes, a Bible institute, college, and/or seminary.

ARTICLE III – ARTICLES OF FAITH

1) THE SCRIPTURES – We believe that the Bible is the Word of God; that it was written by men who were moved by the Holy Spirit so that their

writings, in the original, were supernaturally and verbally inspired and free from error, as no other writings have ever been or ever will be. They are the complete and final revelation of the will of God to man, and so are the supreme authority in all matters of faith and conduct. In the English language, the Word of God is preserved in the King James Version of the Bible.

2) THE TRUE GOD – We believe in one God, eternally existing in three persons, Father, Son, and Holy Spirit.

   a) God the Father – We believe in God the Father, perfect in holiness, boundless in love, infinite in wisdom, measureless in power. We believe that He concerns Himself mercifully in the affairs of men, that He hears and answers prayers, and that He saves from sin and death all that come to Him through Jesus Christ, His son.

   b) God the Son – We believe in Jesus Christ, God the Son, pre-existent with the Father begotten by the Holy Spirit and born of Mary, a virgin; sinless in His nature and life, infallible in His teaching, making atonement for the sins of the world by His substitutionary death on the cross. We believe in His bodily resurrection, His ascension into Heaven, His perpetual intercession for His people and His glorious second advent according to promise. We believe that the promise of His second coming includes: first, "The Blessed Hope" of the believer, namely, the personal, premillenial and pretribulation return of our Lord and Saviour, Jesus Christ, to rapture His church according to 1 Thess. 4:13-18; Second, His return with His saints to set up His millennial reign.

   c) God the Holy Spirit – We believe in the deity and personality of the Holy Spirit. We believe that He came from God to convince and convict the world of sin, of righteousness and of judgment: and to regenerate, sanctify, indwell, and comfort and empower those who believe in Jesus Christ. He always seeks to glorify Jesus Christ.

3) MAN – We believe that man was created in the image of God; that he sinned and thereby incurred not only physical death, but also that spiritual death which is separation from God. We believe that all human beings are born with a sinful nature and in the case of those who reach moral responsibility, become sinners in thought and deed by choice.

4) SATAN – We believe in the reality and personality of Satan.

CHAPTER 8: THE ORGANIZATION OF THE LOCAL CHURCH

5) SALVATION – We believe that the Lord Jesus Christ died for our sins according to the Scriptures, as a representative and substitutionary sacrifice, and that all who by faith receive Him as their personal Saviour, are justified on the grounds of His blood shed on Calvary and His resurrection from the dead and are born again of the Holy Spirit and thereby become the children of God.

6) THE CHURCH – We believe in the visible local church, which is a company of believers in Jesus Christ, baptized on a credible confession of faith, and associated for worship, work, and fellowship. We believe that to these visible churches was committed for perpetual observance, two ordinances; the baptism of believers by immersion and the Lord's Supper. We believe that God has laid upon these churches the task of preaching the Gospel to every creature, and the edification of the individual members of the Body of Christ.

7) LAST THINGS – We believe in the bodily resurrection of all the dead, the saved to eternal life and blessedness in Heaven and the unsaved to eternal, conscious suffering and woe in Hell (John 5:29).

8) ASSURANCE – We believe in the eternal security of the believer (John 10:27-29)

9) CHURCH AND STATE - We believe that every human being has direct relations with God, and is responsible to God alone in all matters of all faith; that each church is independent and autonomous, and must be free from any interference by an ecclesiastical or political authority; that, therefore, the church and state must be kept separate as having different functions, each fulfilling its duties free from the dictation or patronage of the other.

10) CHRISTIAN LIVING – We believe that every saved person should manifest the Christ-life in a consistent walk in the Holy Spirit, fully and constantly yielding his members to the indwelling Christ, so that he may always be by life and word showing forth the praises of him who has called him out of darkness into His marvelous light. We believe in a separated life for all believers as set forth in 2 Cor. 6:14-7:1, including separation from mixed marriages and worldly alliances, pleasures, methods of work, worldly societies, etc.

   NOTE: You may add Scripture if you feel this is necessary.

ARTICLE IV – CHURCH COVENANT

Most covenants are good…depending on how you plan to use them and what you plan to include on discipline.

ARTICLE V – MEMBERSHIP

SECTION 1. RECEPTION OF MEMBERS

(A) By Baptism, upon profession of their faith in Jesus Christ as Saviour and Lord and by accepting the Articles of Faith and the Church Covenant, upon baptism, are received into the membership.

(B) By letter, from another Baptist church of like faith and practice.

(C) By statement, have already professed Jesus as Saviour and having been scripturally baptized (immersed), by another church of like faith and practice.

(D) By restoration, Excluded members may be restored to membership on confession of their error and giving evidence of repentance.

SECTION 2. PROCEDURE FOR MEMBERSHIP

Every candidate for admission to the church shall relate his or her Christian experience to the membership of the church for a vote.

SECTION 3. DISMISSAL FROM MEMBERSHIP

(A) Death

(B) Transfer a member leaving this church for good and proper reasons may be granted, by vote of the church, a letter of transfer to unite with another Baptist church of like faith and practice.

(C) Discipline is that procedure including Christian teaching, training, admonition, and rebuke both private and public, with the view to helping the individual grow in grace, mature in the individual faith, break off from worldliness, and live wholly for the Lord. At such time that a member shall refuse to receive such help it will be necessary for the church to exclude him from the membership.

CHAPTER 8: THE ORGANIZATION OF THE LOCAL CHURCH

Section 1. Differences between individuals or sins not generally known, the wronged party shall follow Matthew 18:15-17. A person bringing a matter into the public or before the church before following this scripture shall be subject to rebuke.

(D) Matters of formal accusation shall be:

1. Public sins or sins known by the church or the general public.

2. Holding and persistently propagating false doctrine.

3. Any failure to abide by the church covenant; such as failure to attend the three weekly services without reasonable excuse, failure to contribute to the church, failure to be reconciled to another member, etc.

Note the following suggestions may need reviewing and revision.

Section 4. Charges must be made in writing, signed, and presented to the church clerk. The church clerk shall give at least one week's notice in writing, with charges stated, to the accused member to appear at a designated meeting for a hearing. If the accused member fails to appear the church may proceed. The accused may call to his aid another church member to speak for him.

Section 5. A member formally accused is automatically released from any office or position, cannot speak at business meetings except at the hearing, and is deprived of his right of vote.

Section 6. At the close of the hearing, the congregation shall vote, by ballot to determine if the accused is guilty. If the accused is found guilty he must be excluded even if he repents. The statement of exclusion, including reasons and admonitions, should be presented to the excluded in person. After time has elapsed and his repentance is proven to be genuine he may again apply for membership.

Section 7. An excluded member can be received back into membership only after repentance and public confession of the sin(s) and following the constitutional procedure for being admitted.

SECTION 4. DUTIES OF MEMBERS – You might consider this if necessary

ARTICLE VI – ORGANIZATION

SECTION 1. The government of this church is vested in the membership.

SECTION 2. The officers of this church shall be pastors and deacons.

SECTION 3. PASTOR

(1) The duties of the pastor shall be the spiritual oversight of the church.

(2) The qualifications of the pastor are those given in 1 Timothy 3:1-7; Titus 1:5-9 and Acts 6:4.

(3) The pastor shall have the ex-officio representation in all organizations and committees. The pastor shall act as the Moderator in all meetings of the church unless the church is without a pastor, at which time the deacons will elect a Chairman that shall preside.

(4) The pastor shall be called for an indefinite term, which shall terminate upon thirty days written notice by either the pastor or the church.

(5) In the event the church is without a pastor the deacons shall act as a Pulpit Committee.

SECTION 4. DEACONS

(1) The duties of the deacons are to be servants to the pastor and the church.

(2) The qualifications of the deacons are those found in Acts 6:1-7 and 1 Timothy 3:8-13

(3) The term of office for a deacon shall be three years at which time they may be re-elected if qualified.

(4) The following officers shall be elected from among the deacons:

   (a) Church clerk

CHAPTER 8: THE ORGANIZATION OF THE LOCAL CHURCH

(b) Church treasurer

(c) Financial secretary

(d) Head usher

ARTICLE VII – MEETINGS AND ELECTIONS

SECTION 1.

The church shall hold its regular monthly business meeting the second Wednesday of each month.

SECTION 2.

The annual meeting shall be held the third Wednesday of January.

SECTION 3.

Special meetings may be called by the pastor, the deacons (when the church is without a pastor) or at the written request of ten voting members. Notice of the special meeting must be given from the pulpit for two consecutive meeting days.

SECTION 4.

Those members ___ years old and over may vote. Any member who has been absent for ___ consecutive Sundays is not eligible to vote.

SECTION 5.

Quorum ___% of the voting membership shall constitute a quorum at any meeting. A ___% majority of the voting members voting at a meeting shall be necessary to carry action except in the case of calling or dismissing a pastor, buying, selling or encumbering property, then ___% of the voting members shall constitute a quorum with ___% majority vote.

SECTION 6.

Except where it is contrary to this Constitution, Roberts Rules of Order shall govern the conduct of the business meeting.

ARTICLE VIII – AUXILIARY ORGANIZATIONS

SECTION 1.

No auxiliary group shall organize without receiving authority from the church.

ARTICLE IX – AMENDMENTS

This Constitution may be amended at any regular business meeting, providing notice has been given of the anticipated amendment at ___ regular services of the church and also that the proposed changes have been conspicuously posted in the church ___ weeks in advance.

ARTICLE X – DISSOLUTION

In the event of dissolution of this organization, proceeds shall be used for a non-profit organization chosen by the membership that meets the requirements of the Internal Revenue Code Section 501 (c) 1943.

NOTE: This sample constitution has been provided by:

Grant Rice

CHAPTER 8: THE ORGANIZATION OF THE LOCAL CHURCH

Sample Document #5

SAMPLE LETTER CALLING FOR A RECOGNITION COUNCIL

Date of letter

First Baptist Church

Main Street

USA

Dear Brethren:

Being a company of immersed believers who have organized ourselves into a local independent Baptist church on (date of organizational meeting) and desiring to have fellowship with other churches of like faith and order, we invite you to send your pastor and two brethren to sit in council on (date of recognition meeting) at the (name and location where the meeting will be held) to consider the propriety of recognizing us as a duly organized Baptist church.

The council will convene at (time).

The following churches and individuals have been invited: (List the names of churches, individuals, and their addresses.)

We are enclosing copies of our charter, covenant, constitution, and articles of faith for you to examine prior to the meeting of the recognition council.

Done by order of and in behalf of the church.

(Name of the church)

(Address)

_____

(Church clerk)

Agenda for a Recognition Council

1. Congregational Song:

2. Prayer

3. Reading of the letter calling for a recognition council

4. Motion to convene the recognition council

5. Election of a moderator

6. Election of a clerk

7. Roll call of churches and individuals invited

8. Motion to seat messengers and other visitors

9. History of the new church (pastor or representative of the new church)

10. Reading of the Church Covenant (questions & answers)

11. Reading of the Church Constitution (questions & answers)

12. Reading of the Church's Articles of Faith (questions & answers)

13. Council moves into executive session for discussion

14. Motion to approve the recognition of the new church

15. Right hand of fellowship extended to the new church

16. Motion to adjourn and dissolve the council

CHAPTER 8: THE ORGANIZATION OF THE LOCAL CHURCH

RECOGNITION SERVICE

1. Congregational Song: Hymn # ....

2. Opening Prayer

3. Report of Council Action by Moderator

4. Scripture Reading: I Timothy 3:1-16

5. Charge to the Church

6. Prayer: Commending the Church to God

7. Congregational Song: Hymn #...

8. Charge to the Church

9. Congregational Song: Hymn #...

10. Message

11. Benediction

(Use visiting pastors or guest speakers for the various responsibilities.)

CHAPTER NINE

THE ADMINISTRATION OF A NEW TESTAMENT BAPTIST CHURCH

By this time, the church planter has moved to his field of service and has started the new church. As the ministry begins to grow, he finds need to have a certain administrative structure in order. This requires leadership and decision concerning administrative policy. Consider the following:

"Everything rises and falls on leadership." (Dr. Lee Roberson)

The importance of pastoral leadership cannot be over emphasized.

After a few weeks into the establishment of the new church, the excitement can fade, the visiting helpers may leave, and the church planter may find himself alone with all the responsibilities of keeping the work growing and running smoothly. PREPARE YOURSELF FOR THIS TIME. The church planter needs to understand ahead of time that the new ministry is going to, more than likely, have its ups and downs. There will be times of great victory with souls being saved and lives being transformed, but there will also be times when nothing seems to be happening, and the church members seem to be moving backwards. The church planter, as pastor and God given "overseer," needs to encourage and strengthen himself and his people in the "grace of the Lord."

"Thou therefore, my son, be strong in the grace that is in Christ Jesus." (2 Timothy 2:1)

CHAPTER 9: THE ADMINISTRATION OF A NT BAPTIST CHURCH

The pastor has been given to the church by the Lord (Ephesians 4:11) and placed in the work by the Holy Spirit to be "overseer" (Acts 20:28) and chief administrator. The people naturally look to him for "leadership." They are, indeed, commanded to do so.

> *"Remember them which have rule over you, who have spoken unto you the word of God: whose faith follow, considering the end of their conversation."* (Hebrews 13:7)
>
> *"Obey them that have the rule over you, and submit yourselves: for they watch for your souls, as they that must give account, that they may do it with joy, and not with grief: for that is unprofitable for you."* (Hebrews 13:17)

The church planter must provide leadership at all times. His leadership will be seen in his ability to: plan, organize, delegate, and coordinate the work of the new church. He must keep his burden for souls, his vision for the ministry, and continually communicate these to his people.

SET GOALS

Setting goals will help you know where you are, where you are going, and how you are going to get there. (The books "Developing The Leader Within You" and "The Winning Attitude" by John C. Maxwell have some very good guidelines for setting and achieving goals). There are also some very helpful books produced by Striving Together Publications. Dr. Paul Chappell is the Pastor of the Lancaster Baptist Church and Founder of the West Coast Baptist College. You can be sure that the writings of Dr. Chappell offer truly biblical principles and that the principles are proven by his personal experience. Books offered by The Old Paths Publications.com of Cleveland, GA are sound and helpful.

Goals allow you to define your priorities and measure your progress. If you have no set goal, how will you know when you get to where it was you wanted to be? If you aim at nothing, you will hit it every time.

Things that help:

1. Write down your goals. Keep them before you and your people.

2. Set realistic, flexible, and measurable goals.

3. Goals should be achievable, yet challengingly high.

4. Goals should have "dates by which to be achieved."

5. Have short term, as well as long range goals.

6. A calendar of events that will contribute to the achieving of your goals will be of benefit.

7. When goals are reached, say so. What has been accomplished? This is why it is good to have anniversary services, etc. Recognize where you were, where you are, and where you desire to be.

8. If goals have not been reached, ask why? When dealing with this issue, be cautious about wounding the spirit of a worker that might have done his/her best but were not able, even at his/her best, to meet the goal. **You should always be more concerned about developing people into mature, effective servants of God than about reaching a secondary goal.** (Hebrews 13:17b, Ephesians 4:12-13)

CHAPTER 9: THE ADMINISTRATION OF A NT BAPTIST CHURCH

<u>Each man of God is different.</u> Some are more methodical and organized than others. <u>Recognize who you are</u> and what works for you as an individual. You will be extremely frustrated and very possibly fail in your ministry if you don't understand this principle. You should recognize your weaknesses. <u>Work at strengthening yourself and at improving yourself</u>. Don't excuse a defect by saying, "That's just the way I am." (Romans 12:1-2)

There is another factor that has to be brought to bear in this matter of administration. The fact is, the various <u>fields of the world differ</u>. Of necessity, <u>some ministries will require more or less administrative structure.</u> The church planter in a village in the jungle of South America will obviously find that his new church will require less or a different structure than that of a missionary planting a church in a metropolitan area.

Business Meetings

Though the "government" of a New Testament Baptist Church should be a "Theocracy" (God rule), we find that the New Testament example is of a "Democracy." Each member should seek to know God's will in each matter having to do with the church and then vote according to that "will" when participating in the business sessions (conference, meeting). "Voice and vote" are two of the privileges afforded the baptized members, in good standing, in the average New Testament Baptist church.

There are extremes when dealing with this issue. There are pastors and church planters that believe they have the right, under God, to make all decisions without regard for the input of the congregation. There is wisdom in the pastor and/or pastor and deacons having the church-given authority to make certain decisions without calling a "conference." The people of the church should have the right to participate in the decision-making process in matters of significance (sizable expenditures, the calling of staff members, supporting of missionaries, etc.). In most cases, strong leadership is desirable. If the leadership is "too" strong, it could be a hindrance to the development of new leadership in the congregation. **The church planter, especially, should be striving to train capable men and women to fill places of Biblical leadership from day one.**

The other extreme is when, over the course of time, the pastor has been reduced to the position of "puppet." The congregation and/or the deacons make all the decisions. The pastor is only there to see that these decisions are carried out. This situation is unscriptural. Unfortunately, some churches have this policy due to past abuses by dictatorial pastors.

CHAPTER 9: THE ADMINISTRATION OF A NT BAPTIST CHURCH

The church planter can avoid both extremes by developing a ministry that follows the New Testament example of strong servant leadership both in the pulpit and the pew.

The decision concerning the number or frequency of business meetings will be determined by the need for them. In churches that are incorporated the law requires at least one business meeting a year.

The business meeting affords the opportunity for regular reports (financial and otherwise), decisions in matters of the church ministry, granting of church letters, elections, etc. The church planter has the opportunity to train his people so that they have the right attitude toward the business meeting. The business meeting can be a time of blessing and unity. **Usually problems come when there is prayerlessness, self-will, and power struggles. Holy Ghost-filled people don't allow any of these three to dominate their lives.**

The church planter/pastor should prepare for business meetings by discussing ahead of time, with the deacons and other leaders of the church, the matters to be presented in the session. If there is not unity or agreement among the leaders, there will more than likely not be among the congregation. Use wisdom. **Respect the opinion of your leaders.** Wisely table matters that may cause conflict until they can be bathed in prayer. God is able to do a work. Give place to Him. Make decisions on the basis of what your purposes are. If we do this will it help us accomplish our purpose? The Lord is not the author of confusion.

Print and distribute all reports prior to the meeting. Do not read the printed reports. Keep things moving.

The pastor should moderate all business meetings. In absence of a pastor, the designated deacon or someone selected by the church can fill the post of moderator.

Business meetings should be announced prior to the fact, except for some cases that involve voting to meet some immediate need. A church is less likely to make bad decisions if time is allowed for prayerful consideration of the matters at hand.

THE PROPER ORDER:

1. Open with prayer.

2. The business meeting must be called to order.

3. The minutes of the previous meeting are read.

    (If the minutes are printed and distributed beforehand it is not necessary to read them. Minutes approved.

4. Reports are given.

5. Discussion of any unfinished business.

6. Presentation, discussion, and decisions, concerning new business.

7. Adjournment.

What quorum is required for voting on an issue?

Who may express opinions?

Who may vote?

CHAPTER 9: THE ADMINISTRATION OF A NT BAPTIST CHURCH

It would be good for the church planter to have the Bible and a copy of "Robert's Rules of Order" available

PASTORS and DEACONS

Pastors (Elders, Bishops) and Deacons: Qualifications

1Timothy 3:1-13, Acts 6:1-7

A. <u>Blameless</u> (1 Timothy 3:2) means "nothing to take hold upon" – that is, there must be nothing in his life that Satan or the unsaved can take hold of to criticize or attack the church. No man on earth today is sinless, but we must strive to be above reproach.

B. <u>Husband of one wife</u> (vs. 2). The office of "pastor" or of "deacon" is not given to a woman. This expression also means that a pastor and/or deacon must not be divorced and/or remarried. A man's ability to manage his marriage and home indicates that he probably has the ability to oversee a local church. Dedicated Christians who have been divorced and/or remarried may serve in other offices in the local church, but they are disqualified from being pastors, elders (teaching adults) or deacons.

C. <u>Vigilant</u> (vs. 2) means temperate or sober. This is the ability to keep one's head in all situations. It is to be able to exercise sensible judgment in all things.

D. <u>Sober</u> (vs.2) means he does not cheapen the ministry by foolish behavior. He is a serious person and earnest about his work. He should have a sense of humor, however.

E. <u>Of good behavior</u>. This can be understood as orderly or organized.

F. <u>Given to hospitality</u> (vs. 2). "Loving the stranger." Open and friendly.

G. <u>Apt to teach</u> (vs. 2). The pastor and deacons as leaders of the church should be able to teach. For one to be a good teacher, he must first be a good student.

H. <u>Not given to wine</u> (vs. 3). The pastor and deacons must not give themselves to the use of alcoholic beverages. Wine was used for medicinal purposes in Christ's day. Some medicines today contain alcohol but there is a definite difference between social and medicinal purposes.

I. <u>No striker</u> (vs. 3). "Not contentious", not looking for a fight (verbal or otherwise).

J. <u>Not greedy of filthy lucre</u> (vs.3). The man that sees the ministry as a means to make money is disqualified.

K. <u>Patient</u> (vs.3). Gentle, willing to listen, able to take criticism without reacting in an unchristian manner.

L. <u>Not a brawler</u> (vs.3) a peacemaker, not one that stirs up trouble. One that can disagree without being disagreeable. Short tempers lead to short ministries.

M. <u>Not covetous</u> (vs.3) of money, fame, etc.

N. <u>A godly family</u> (vss. 4-5). Not necessary to be married or have children, but if so, he is to have a consistent testimony at church and at home.

O. <u>Not a novice</u> (vs.6) literally means, "One newly planted" as in reference to a new Christian.

CHAPTER 9: THE ADMINISTRATION OF A NT BAPTIST CHURCH

P. <u>A good testimony outside the church</u> (vs.7). He should have a good reputation with the saved and unsaved with which he does business. Good character.

The election of the first deacons (Greek word meaning "servant") is recorded in Acts, chapter six. In the church today, deacons should assist and relieve the pastor of certain tasks so that he may, concentrate on the ministry of the Word, prayer, and spiritual oversight of the ministry. Though the deacons are not assigned the same authority or responsibilities as the pastor, they should meet basically the same qualifications.

A. Acts 6:3 states they were to be chosen from the congregation, men of honest report, and full of the Holy Ghost and wisdom. Such men were effective witnesses for the Lord. (1 Timothy 3:8-13

B. Grave (vs.8). Worthy of respect. He is to use the office to serve, not just fill it.

C. Not double-tongued (vs.8) not a gossip. Not a liar.

D. Not given to much wine (vs. 8).

E. Not greedy of filthy lucre (vs. 8). Deacons handle church funds and should be above reproach. A spiritual attitude toward money is necessary.

F. Doctrinally sound (vs. 9). The word "mystery" means truth once hidden but now revealed by God. Deacons must understand Christian doctrine and obey it with a good conscience. Decisions must be based on the Word of God, not personal preference, or opinion. A deacon should know and understand the spirit and letter of the church's by-laws, but it is more important that he know and live the Word of God.

G. Tested and proven (vs. 10). An untested Christian man is an unprepared Christian.

H. Godly home (vss. 11-12). The deacon's wife must also be qualified, or she will disqualify her husband.

I. A willingness to work (vs. 13), not rule.

Note: As the years pass it is increasingly difficult to find men that are biblically qualified for the offices of pastors and deacons. Do not use this as an excuse to compromise His Word.

<u>No one in the church is perfect, but a man and his wife should meet these basic qualifications.</u> Each of us should strive to qualify. Those who cannot qualify should not look at that as reason to drop out or do nothing in the service of the Lord. Some will not be able to meet these qualifications but will certainly be able to serve in some other area of the local church. May the older generation seek to set an example before the young and challenge them to give their lives to the Lord for unrestricted service. As we allow God to work in us, He will be able to work through us.

Deacons should always:

1) Be faithful to the church.

   a. Attending all services

   b. Supporting it with tithes and offerings

   c. Promoting it's welfare and growth

   d. Praying for it

2) Be loyal to the Pastor and Members.

3) Be vigilant concerning the needs of the individual member and the congregation as a whole.

4) Be an example for all both young and old, to follow.

5) Be faithful to his family.

6) Have a consistent prayer life.

7) Make every effort to increase his knowledge of the Bible.

8) Be filled with the Holy Spirit

Being controlled by the Holy Spirit will cause a man to be a witness for Christ and manifest the fruit of the Spirit as found in Galatians 5:22 (love, joy, peace, longsuffering, gentleness, goodness, faith, meekness, temperance).

The Duties of a Deacon

1) The deacons are the pastor's helpers. It should never be forgotten why the first deacons were elected by the church. Again, we are told in Acts 6:1-3 that the deacons were elected to take certain burdens off of the pastors.

2) The deacons help in the work with the shut-ins and widows.

3) The deacons form an advisory board. The board has no authority to run the church. <u>Final authority rests with the church.</u> The pastor and deacons can discuss plans for the future of the church and prayerfully consider the direction in which it should go, but they must present these recommendations to the congregation for approval.

4) At least one deacon is elected to serve as a trustee.

5) Deacons and their wives should be prepared to do personal work at the altar during the invitation in all services. The deacons and their wives should come during the invitation with Bible in hand and be ready to lead the lost that respond to accept Christ. They may also need to pray with a Christian that comes forward.

6) The deacons should oversee the collection of offerings, the counting, recording of amounts, and deposit of such.

7) The deacons should prepare the baptistry for baptisms and with their wives be of any assistance that is necessary.

8) The deacons should prepare the elements and table for the observance of the Lord's Supper, as well as take part with the pastor in serving the same.

9) The deacons should see as their responsibility the cares and concerns of the church in matters dealing with material things so as to relieve (not isolate) the pastor or pastors of these concerns.

10) The deacons along with the pastors constitute the committee for discipline but also for praying over the sick.

11) The deacons and pastors make up the nominating committee.

12) It is good for the deacons to visit the sick and prospects.

13) The deacons should inform the pastor of anything that could have negative results on the ministry.

CHAPTER 9: THE ADMINISTRATION OF A NT BAPTIST CHURCH

The church planter will have to teach and train men and women to serve in these official capacities if the church is to have this benefit. The church planter's leadership in training these leaders is crucial.

CHURCH WORKERS

God places gifted people in the church to meet the needs of the local congregation. As a church planter, you will need to help folk discover their gifts and talents and then direct them in the exercise and use of those gifts and talents to honor Christ in the church.

GUIDELINES:

1. Use caution. (I Timothy 5:22)

2. **Set qualifications and standards in the beginning of the work.** Teach your people the importance of setting a high standard for those involved in public service in the church. It is a privilege to serve God but also a great responsibility. Teach the truths of 1 Corinthians 9:19-27.

   "For though I be free from all men, yet have I made myself servant unto all, that I might gain the more." (1 Corinthians 9:19)

   (See leadership covenant)

3. **Recruit workers rather than ask for volunteers.** As pastor, you should get to know the people before approaching them about a position. Sometimes, it is wise to appoint an individual to a task on a temporary basis.

4. Workers should be appointed by pastor and deacons rather than elected by the church or at least recommended by them.

5. **Train** your workers so that they know what is expected of them. Provide for **evaluation** of their work. **Help** them "grow into" their job.

6. **Correct,** reprimand or replace workers in a Christian manner. Do not gossip or belittle them publicly. Set high ethical standards for yourself and your workers.

7. **Communicate** with your workers. They are vital to the ministry and should feel the part and know you care for them.

8. The idea is to **build lives.** For this one must have patience and a persevering spirit.

9. **Reward** your workers

THE "TEAM" CONCEPT IN CHURCH PLANTING

There are obvious reasons why it is a great advantage to work as a team in church planting. There must be open and honest discussion about key matters.

GUIDELINES:

1. Prayerfully develop a **written agreement,** which delineates the responsibilities of each team member. Who will do what? Recognize each other's spiritual gifts. One may do most of the public preaching while the other concentrates on private evangelism and discipleship of converts. One may administer the Sunday school while

CHAPTER 9: THE ADMINISTRATION OF A NT BAPTIST CHURCH

the other heads the youth or music ministry of the church. Allow your partner to minister where he or she feels comfortable and can be the most effective. At the same time, there must be a willingness, on the part of the team members, to help out in areas where help is needed.

2. **Determine how much** time and money will be contributed by each member of the team. This may differ since responsibilities, income, and physical capabilities vary. A minimum should be agreed upon to avoid resentment or misunderstandings. If you can do more, great!

3. **Decide who is going to be the leader.** Usually one will have greater administrative abilities. This does not mean he will "run the show." Both must recognize that neither is boss. But for the sake of the work, a chain of command must be established. **Be loyal to one another.**

4. Establish a regular time for planning, praying, reporting, evaluating, setting of goals, and problem solving each week. **Discuss problems and differences as soon as they arise.** Do not ignore them or hope they will go away. If genuine areas of disagreement exist. Use the Word of God as the final authority. Include your wives in this planning and praying as much as possible.

5. **Determine to build up your partner.** Never criticize him or her to the members of the congregation. Never question your partner's teaching or actions publicly. Discuss them with him or her privately at a later time.

6. If a single lady is part of the team, be careful not to abuse her gifts, demand too much of her, or expect her to provide you with free babysitting. She needs time to herself just as the other members of the team do. Allow her to exercise her gifts fully within biblical parameters.

7. Record the entire agreement in writing so there will not be misunderstandings later. Too often people forget what was promised or remember things differently at a later date.

From the very beginning of the new church the church planter should state, review, repeat and hold up before the people the Scriptural objectives of the ministry...to win the lost, to disciple new convert, to train the members, to promote oneness (fellowship) in Christ and last but not least to worship God. Those becoming a part of the church will need to be committed to these goals. Though nothing more than their attendance to the services can be expected from the lost – **much can be expected of the members and even more form the leaders.**

Those desiring to serve in places of leadership must be willing to live to a higher standard.

The Scripture is a life changing agent. The missionary church planter is also an agent of change. Once a person has been converted it is reasonable to expect changes in his life. The Scripture calls these changes "sanctification" or as in Romans 12:1-2, "transformation."

The fact is God has predetermined that saved people be conformed, not to the world's mold but to the "image of Christ." Do not hesitate to preach this important truth.

SAMPLE #6

A LEADERSHIP COVENANT

Having received Jesus Christ as my personal Savior and being an active member, in good standing of this church, I recognize the privilege that is mine to serve in a leadership position. I realize that it is my duty to be "an example to believers, in word, in conversation, in charity, in spirit, in faith, in purity." Therefore, I promise that with the aid of the Holy Spirit I will strive to fulfill my leadership responsibilities and to abide by the following covenant:

1. I readily subscribe to the doctrinal position, the policies, and program of my church and will support them both publicly and privately.

2. I will faithfully attend the regular services of my church including Sunday School, Sunday Morning and Evening Services and Prayer Meeting and all other meetings that may be expected of me as a leader in this church, unless providentially hindered.

3. I will support the ministry of our church through my prayers, presence, and finances.

4. I will be loyal to my pastor. I will cooperate with him, pray for him, and seek to encourage him as we labor together.

5. I will be exemplary in my conduct, not using tobacco, alcohol, or illicit drugs and will dress appropriately for all services and activities.

6. I will seek to fulfill my responsibilities on time and in accordance with the instructions I am given.

7. If for some reason I cannot fulfill my obligations, I will notify the appropriate leaders and will cooperate fully in seeking a replacement.

Name:_____

Date:_____

It is left to the conviction and discretion of the individual church planter to amplify and/or incorporate a "leadership covenant." Having such a covenant establishes biblical standards and guidelines that can serve as a constant reminder of the responsibilities of those in roles of leadership.

CHAPTER 9: THE ADMINISTRATION OF A NT BAPTIST CHURCH

THE SERVICES OF THE CHURCH
(WORSHIP, PRAYER MEETINGS, ETC.)

The church planter will most likely pattern the services of his new church after those of his home church. This is normal. Each church takes on a certain personality, usually that of the pastor/church planter. There are some elements to remember:

1. The services should afford opportunities for <u>worship, instruction, fellowship, and evangelism</u>. Putting it another way, this means **Exaltation of the Lord, Edification of the believers, and Evangelization of the lost.**

2. The services should be <u>regular</u>. (Hebrews 10:25) Middle class American culture says the church should meet Sunday A.M. & P.M. and on Wednesday P.M. for prayer meeting. Scripturally any or every day of the week is appropriate for service. You do need to teach your people the important principle of "setting aside time each week" for the specific purpose of worshiping God. The early disciples observed the custom of meeting on Sunday (John 20:19). New converts should be taught the value of meeting several times a week: to hear sound preaching, to study the Bible, for receiving encouragement and strength through fellowship, to worship the Lord and edify one another through the singing of hymns and spiritual songs and prayer, and also to have greater opportunities to invite the lost. Note: Sunday is not the Sabbath; it is the first day of the week.

3. <u>Cultivate true worship.</u> Guard against the worship service becoming a "show or spectacle." The Lord is the object of worship. Focus on Him.

4. <u>Involve your people</u> in the services of the church. The men can read Scripture and pray while others can sing

and give testimonies, etc. Use the young people in the services.

5. <u>Make every service as important as the other</u>. Have special music on Wednesday night, etc. If you downplay the midweek service, your people will think it is not as important.

6. <u>A nursery</u> can be a blessing if done correctly. Crying babies often distract from the service. Exercise caution. It is better to have a crying baby and his/her parents in the service than to have neither.

7. <u>Children's church</u> can also be a blessing, but it should be "church," not just fun and games. It should be on their level and geared to keep their attention. At a certain age, children should join their parents in the regular church service.

8. <u>Special meetings</u> should be planned each year. You will want to have a missions conference, revival, Bible conference, soul-winning conference, etc. Each special meeting should contribute to the goals that you have for the church. Plan well, publicize, promote, and PRAY. Plan ahead to meet the expenses of the meetings. Make them something positive.

Note:

Be a blessing to the guest speakers, the missionaries, evangelists and their families. Pay their expenses and give a love offering as an expression of appreciation and to meet specific needs.

It is important to take great care concerning who is allowed to sing, give testimony, teach, or preach from the

CHAPTER 9: THE ADMINISTRATION OF A NT BAPTIST CHURCH

platform or from behind the pulpit. If you invite someone, allow them this opportunity, and then discover afterwards that they were not worthy or someone you would invite again, you may have already done damage. Invariably someone in the congregation will be impressed with the individual or group and think that they should be invited back. The average church member does not always have the spiritual discernment in these matters.

9. <u>Youth ministries</u> are essential. Fun, food, and fellowship are three things teens enjoy, but they can also be challenged to serve the Lord. Often they will become some of your best workers.

10. <u>Music ministries</u> play a very important role in the establishment of a new church. You will have to guard against the entrance of worldly music into the church. This is a point of much controversy today. Often, worldly music is used to attract the lost and the carnal. Care must be taken to avoid pleasing the "flesh" at risk of grieving the Holy Spirit.

> *"Let the word of Christ dwell in you richly in all wisdom; teaching and admonishing one another in psalms and hymns and spiritual songs, singing with grace in your hearts to the Lord."* (Colossians 3:16)

11. <u>Church ordinances</u>

Baptism is the first step of obedience for every new believer. In the New Testament, Paul is the only example we have of anyone waiting three days after their conversion to be baptized. In all other cases, new believers were baptized the same day. The candidate for baptism needs to understand salvation and the significance of baptism before being baptized. Baptism is a local church ordinance and should be done under the authority of the local church. Para-church groups have no authority to baptize. Only believers coming into the local church should be baptized.

Some suggest that believers that have unresolved situations in their lives (unmarried couples living together, etc.) should resolve them before being baptized. There might be cases where the individual could be baptized and accepted as a member of the church but with no member privileges (voice, vote, accept position of service, etc.) until the problems are resolved. This would be a rare situation. Have baptismal certificates prepared beforehand.

New churches without baptismal pools will need to secure permission to use one at another church or to baptize in the river, in the ocean, in a pond, or even a swimming pool.

The formula:

"Upon your profession of faith in Jesus Christ as Lord and Saviour, and in obedience to His command, I baptize you, my (brother, or sister) in the name of the Father, of the Son and of the Holy Ghost."

Note:

The mode of baptism must be according to Scripture, but so must the "baptizer." A person baptized under the authority of a church that does not have sound Bible doctrine should be re-baptized before being accepted as a member in a Baptist church. The mode, the motive (not unto salvation as some groups say), the authority (the local Baptist church), and the person doing the baptizing must all meet scriptural standards.

The Lord's Supper: In Acts 2:42; we are told that the early disciples "continued steadfastly in the apostles' doctrine and fellowship and in the breaking of bread and in prayers. The "breaking of bread" speaks of the Lord's Supper. This second ordinance of the local church should be celebrated with solemnity, as a time for remembrance, repentance, and rededication. The focus should be on Christ and His death in our place on the cross but specifically on his body and blood that were offered for us. The guidelines for the pastor to follow in presiding over the Lord's Supper are found in 1 Corinthians 11:23-34. The Lord's Supper is for believers only. The church planter will decide if the Supper is "**Closed** (only baptized members of the local congregation), **Close** (baptized believers of churches of like faith) or **Open** (anyone professing faith in Jesus Christ)." It should be remembered that it is a local church ordinance and that there are grave consequences when taken unworthily.

Note: Fermented wine is not to be used for the Lord's Supper. A distorted picture would be presented of the shed blood of the Lord Jesus Christ if a fermented beverage were used. Because Christ and His disciples were celebrating the Passover feast the night the Lord instituted His Supper, all of the elements (the bread and the fruit of the vine) were to be free of leaven. Leaven as an agent of fermentation was a "type" of sin. It should be remembered that the wine of Jesus day on contained 3%-4% alcohol. That of today contains 60%-80%.

It should also be noted that the word "wine" is not used in reference to the Lord's Supper. "The cup" is used in I Corinthians and "the fruit of the vine" is used in Mark 14:25.

12. <u>The Invitation</u>   Charles Hadden Spurgeon warned his disciples: "Brethren, **we must plead**. Entreaties and beseeching must blend with our instructions...In our Master's name we must give the invitation, crying, 'Whosoever will, let him take of the water of life freely.'"

The reading of the book, <u>Lectures to My Students</u> by Charles H. Spurgeon, will benefit all ministerial students.

Every new convert should profess faith in Christ publicly. During the invitation is a great time and place to start. How often we fail in this all-important matter. We cast the net, but are ever so weak in drawing it in. **Do not pressure people but by all means give them the opportunity to respond to Christ and His word.** Be specific in the invitation (to the lost, to the backslider, to the dedicated Christian for service, etc.).

When a person responds to the invitation, ask why they came. See that their need is met (salvation, rededication, surrender, etc.). Train counselors and have them ready and waiting. Talk with each person and pray with each person. Unless it is someone well known by the pastor, make a written note of their name and reason for responding. Place yourself and your helpers at the disposition of those that do not respond publicly.

CHAPTER 9: THE ADMINISTRATION OF A NT BAPTIST CHURCH

SAMPLE #7
SUGGESTED GUIDELINES FOR THE NURSERY WORKERS

1. Consider the nursery a ministry to the Lord and to parents with small children. Your willingness to serve here makes it possible for many others to enjoy the worship service without disruption.

    a. Children should be kept as quiet as possible.

    b. Encourage activities that will not excite the children (story telling, reading, coloring, playing quietly).

    c. To protect small children and babies, no running, jumping, climbing, wrestling, or throwing of toys is to be allowed.

2. Only children under <u>36 months</u> of age should be permitted in the nursery.

    a. Teens, children, and parents should not be allowed in the nursery unless bringing or picking up children.

    b. Discourage people from entering or leaving the church through the nursery. (This disrupts the nursery and is a health hazard.)

3. Be in the nursery at least 15-30 minutes before the beginning of the service and remain until the last child has been picked up by his or her parents.

    a. A "nursery registration" card should be filled out for each child the first time he or she is placed in the nursery.

    b. Have positive identification for each child and parent.

c. Ask for help whenever the ratio of one worker for every three children is exceeded.

d. Remain in the nursery until all children have been picked up by their parents. DO NOT ALLOW THE CHIDREN TO LEAVE ALONE WHEN THE SERVICE IS OVER.

e. Leave the nursery neat and clean. Pick up all toys, paper, and books. Replace things taken from the cabinets. Put diapers in plastic bags and dispose of them.

4. Do not feed the children anything without the parent's permission. NO FOOD SHOULD BE LEFT IN THE NURSERY. Cookies and small snacks may be the exceptions to this rule but they should be stored in air tight, bug proof containers.

5. Know and have a written record of what food allergies exist for each child.

6. Have a safe place for keeping medications. Have a record of what medications are for which child, the dosages, the schedule, etc. Exercise extreme caution in this matter.

7. Remove books and coloring items from the cabinets for the children and replace them neatly on the shelves when finished. Do not allow the children to open cabinets or to throw things back into them.

8. Report to your nursery leader any problems you have.

    a. If you cannot be in the nursery on your assigned Sunday, inform the nursery leader as far in advance as possible.

CHAPTER 9: THE ADMINISTRATION OF A NT BAPTIST CHURCH

    b. Please do not arrange for your own substitute unless instructed to do so by the nursery leader.

9. Only surrender the child to the parent, a guardian or a designated person.

10. Be aware of the "liability factors."

11. Beware of predators…

SAMPLE #8
SUGGESTED GUIDELINES FOR THE NURSERY LEADER

1. Make up a list of nursery workers for each service. Post this schedule in the nursery on the last Sunday of the month and give a copy to your supervisor.

    a. Try to maintain a ratio of one worker for every three children.

    b. Under most circumstances nursery helpers should be at least 12 years old – if helping an adult

    c. Contact nursery workers to remind them when they are scheduled to be in the nursery.

2. Meet with nursery workers once each quarter.

    a. Impress upon your workers that the nursery is a ministry, both to the parents and to the young children. It is not just a baby-sitting job.

    b. Encourage workers to teach Bible truths to toddlers rather than simply letting them play all the time.

    c. Discuss any problems, equipment needs, or supplies.

    d. Keep your supervisor advised of problems and progress.

3. Check on the nursery each Sunday to be sure it is functioning properly.

    a. Only nursery workers should be allowed in the nursery.

    b. Only children 0-36 months should be in the nursery.

CHAPTER 9: THE ADMINISTRATION OF A NT BAPTIST CHURCH

4. Be sure all teaching materials are in agreement with the policy and doctrinal position of the church.

5. Remove broken toys and worn-out books. Have safe toys. Keep equipment in good repair. Keep the cabinets neat and well organized.

6. Empty the wastebasket and dispose of dirty diapers after each service.

    a. Sheets should be washed every week, toys every other week and the cribs at least once a month.

    b. Do not leave food in the nursery.

    c. Maintain a supply of fresh water, moist towelettes, and plastic bags (for soiled diapers) at all times.

7. Inform your workers that the nursery will be open 15-30 minutes before and after the services to encourage fellowship among parents and to alleviate possible pressure on any parents who may wish to respond to the invitation.

    Note: In recent days it has been dangerous for the health of children to have a functioning nursery due to the Corona Virus. Now and in the future special attention should be give in the matter of sanitizing all church facilities and equipment. Special attention should be given to the nursery and Sunday school classrooms.

SUGGESTED SAMPLE #9

SUNDAY SCHOOL WORKER'S COVENANT

Having received Jesus Christ as my personal Savior, and being a baptized member of this church, I acknowledge that I have been afforded the special privilege of teaching the Word of God. In view of my appointment as a Sunday school worker, and relying on the help and guidance of the Holy Spirit, I promise to fulfill my responsibilities and to abide by the following covenant:

1. I readily subscribe to the doctrinal statement of my church and will teach nothing that is in conflict with its position.

2. I will cooperate fully with the educational program of this church, use the materials provided, attend the teachers' meetings, and accept the supervision, advice, and training offered by those in charge.

3. I will set aside time daily for communion with my Lord in prayer and Bible reading.

4. I will faithfully attend and promote the services of my church (Sunday school, Morning Service, Evening Service, and Prayer Meeting) and will support this church through my tithes, offerings, and prayers.

5. I will be exemplary in my conduct, not using tobacco, alcoholic beverages, or illicit drugs and will dress appropriately, to please and honor the Lord Jesus Christ for all services.

6. I will earnestly pray for the conversion of unsaved class members and for the spiritual growth of those who are Christians.

7. I will faithfully prepare each lesson, not waiting until Saturday to begin and will be in my classroom fifteen minutes before Sunday school is to begin. In class I will use the KJV Bible as

CHAPTER 9: THE ADMINISTRATION OF A NT BAPTIST CHURCH

our primary textbook and other materials provided by the church.

8. If at all possible I will contact all visitors and absentees before the following Sunday and will visit in the home of each pupil in my class at least once every six months.

9. I will see each of my students as a "trust" from the Lord and will guard them from harm.

10. If for some reason I must be absent or cannot fulfill my responsibilities, I will notify the chairman of the education committee immediately and will cooperate fully in seeking a replacement rather than seeking my own substitute.

Name: _____

Class: _____

Date: _____

SAMPLE #10
A SERVICE QUESTIONNAIRE FOR CHRISTIAN WORKERS

Please check the areas in which you have had experience:

❑ S.S. Teacher	❑ S.S. Superintendent
❑ Children's Church	❑ Youth Leader
❑ Choir	❑ Visitation
❑ Song Leader	❑ Usher
❑ Special Music	❑ Bus Ministry
❑ Piano/Organ	❑ Bookkeeping
❑ Nursery	❑ Electrical Work
❑ Deacon	❑ Custodian
❑ Artistic Work	❑ Painting
❑ Secretarial Work	❑ Carpentry
❑ Missionary Leader	❑ Other

Please check the areas of ministry in which you are willing to serve, if asked to do so:

❑ S.S. Teacher	❑ S.S. Superintendent
❑ Children's Church	❑ Youth Leader
❑ Choir	❑ Visitation
❑ Song Leader	❑ Usher

CHAPTER 9: THE ADMINISTRATION OF A NT BAPTIST CHURCH

- ☐ Special Music
- ☐ Piano/Organ
- ☐ Nursery
- ☐ Deacon
- ☐ Artistic Work
- ☐ Secretarial Work
- ☐ Missionary Leader

- ☐ Bus Ministry
- ☐ Bookkeeping
- ☐ Electrical Work
- ☐ Custodian
- ☐ Painting
- ☐ Carpentry
- ☐ Other

In some areas of the world this type of questionnaire for Christian workers will be totally impractical.

The Sunday School

The Sunday School (S.S.) can be a great tool for carrying out the second half of the Great Commission.

> *"Teaching them to observe all things whatsoever I have commanded you."* (Matthew 28:20)

The Sunday School can serve two major purposes – that of bringing people to the knowledge of Christ as Lord and Saviour and also that of teaching the believer the truths that are so basic to the Christian life. A well-organized S.S. will minister to the needs of all age groups. The church planter will have to work with three factors. These are as follows:

1. The number of qualified teachers
2. Space available and equipment
3. The number of people enrolled (ages, level of spiritual maturity, etc.)

As qualified teachers and space become available, the S.S. can be divided into at least nine groups.

1. Cradle roll (From newborn babies to two years)
2. Nursery (Two to four years)
3. Beginners (Four years through kindergarten)
4. Primaries (Ages six through eight or 1st-3rd grades)
5. Juniors (Ages nine through eleven or 4th-6th grades)
6. Junior High School (7th-9th grades)

CHAPTER 9: THE ADMINISTRATION OF A NT BAPTIST CHURCH

7. Senior High School (10th-12th grades)

8. Young Adults (Ages eighteen through twenty-four)

9. Adults (Ages twenty-five and up)

The classes for children function better if the number of students is limited to 8-10 in a class. Young people and adult classes can be of almost any size and limited mostly by the size of the classroom. We could discuss at length the requirements for equipment and classrooms, but what would be said would only be the "ideal." Very seldom does the church planter have ideal situations with which to work.

The church planter will need to provide biblically sound materials for his teachers to use, especially if they are new at the job. It may be necessary to go over the lesson with the teachers each week. The same high standards that we have already discussed apply to teachers. The church planter must dedicate time to training teachers.

> *"And the things that thou has heard of me among many witnesses, the same commit thou to faithful men, who shall be able teach others also."* (2 Timothy 2:2)

It may be good to challenge a mature man or woman to start and build a class. Work with them. Help them with initial contacts. Guide them and provide the classroom and materials they will need.

PERSONAL OR ALTAR WORKERS (Deacons, their wives, Sunday School Teachers, Ushers, Bus Workers, etc.)

1. Be present, attentive, and prayerful in every service. Be ready to "come forward" during the invitation.

2. Dress appropriately.

3. Be careful of personal presentation. (Bad breath, body odor, tobacco smell, etc.)

4. Have Bible in hand. Have a note pad, clipboard, and pen with which to write.

5. Be alert to Pastor's signals.

6. It is helpful to ask, "Why have you come?"

7. Generally, people come for salvation, rededication (make things right), or to pray for some particular burden.

8. The best way to know if a person is saved is to ask, "Do you know that if you died right now you would go to heaven?"

9. Lead them to Christ if appropriate. Pray with them.

10. Ask new converts about baptism and church membership.

11. Be sensitive to people's needs.

12. Fill out the inquirers card and give it to the pastor.

13. Remember the "invitation" is not the appropriate time to enter into a lengthy discussion about some doctrinal issue. These issues should be dealt with at a better time and place.

SUNDAY SCHOOL TEACHERS

1. Sunday School teachers should meet the same scriptural standards as the deacon or his wife. These are found in 1 Timothy 3:1-13. (A born again, baptized, active member).

CHAPTER 9: THE ADMINISTRATION OF A NT BAPTIST CHURCH

2. Being a Sunday School teacher is a great privilege that brings with it great responsibility.

3. The teacher's life should be an example for others to follow. Others are going to follow.

4. Teachers should be Spirit-filled because it is impossible to truly communicate the truths and principles of God's Word apart from the work of the Holy Spirit.

5. The teacher should have a working knowledge of the fundamentals of the faith and a desire to increase his or her knowledge of God's Word.

6. The teacher will need to be a good student.

7. The teacher should promote and defend the beliefs and practices of the church as a sacred trust and be loyal to Christ, Pastor, and fellow saints.

8. The teachers should be careful that what they "allow or disallow" not be a cause of stumbling to the student. The teacher should not participate in questionable amusements or activities such as drinking any kind of alcoholic beverage, dancing, gambling, and other habits that are detrimental to the testimony of Jesus Christ and the ministry of the church.

9. The teacher should have a burden for winning souls and a concern for the spiritual growth and welfare of the students.

CHAPTER TEN

MISSIONS: WORLD EVANGELIZATION

<u>**The church planter has not completed his task until the new church is actively involved in world evangelization, through praying, giving, and sending missionaries**</u>. Very early in the life of a new church, there should be support for missionaries. Often it is argued that the church should take care of its own needs first. There should be a balance, but a church, even a new church, should not put off supporting missions until it has "extra" money. Even if the new church is not able to pay the pastor's full salary, it should take on at least one missionary for monthly support. This step of faith is one of the best ways to increase your people's vision and burden for souls at home and abroad.

"As the pastor goes, so goes the church."

If you as the pastor do not have a burden for world evangelization, neither will your people. There are some things that you can do to increase your vision or to develop one.

1. Study the Scripture, especially the book of Acts, with missions in mind.

2. Read great missionary stories.

3. Have missionaries you know come and talk with you and your church people.

4. Read missionary prayer letters.

5. Pray daily for at least one missionary.

CHAPTER 10: MISSIONS: WORLD EVANGELIZATION

6. Visit a foreign field where you support a missionary.

7. Pray for God to work in your heart.

8. Ask yourself where you would be if it were not for churches with a missionary burden and missionaries.

9. Put up a missionary map with pictures of missionaries.

10. Talk with other pastors about their missions programs. (Of course, you want to talk with someone that God is using and not someone overcome by jealousy, bitterness, self-centeredness, etc.)

The church planter may want to have a missions committee. This committee should work with the pastor in formulating **a mission's policy.** The policy will serve as a statement of the goals of the missions program and a guide for selecting missionaries and/or missions projects. Certainly "Baptist money should work for Baptists."

A Missions Committee and Missions Policy are not intended to bind the church, but they can serve the purpose of keeping the Missions Program of the church on course.

Very often decisions are made on a "whim" or based on "emotion." At times, when churches change pastors, the new pastor changes the total missions program of the church. Some have gone so far as to drop all of the missionaries supported by the church. Having a written missions policy in place will help to avoid such unethical practices.

Please note this article written by the late Dr. Ray Thompson.

Developing a Written Church Missions Policy

It is very important for every Baptist church to adopt (*accept formally and put into effect*) a written missions policy. The time and effort it takes to prayerfully compile and publish an approved missions policy will be greatly appreciated by the church body and its missionaries.

There are a number of questions that need to be addressed before drafting a church policy regarding missions and missionary personnel:

1. Who should the church support or not support as missionaries?

2. Which mission boards or agencies should be looked to for assistance in providing the needs of its missionaries as well as needs the church may not be able to provide?

3. Should the church give financial support to fewer missionaries for a larger amount or more missionaries for a smaller amount?

4. As a sending church should more support and assistance be given to members of the church who are missionaries than would be given to missionaries who were commissioned by another sending church?

5. What special things should the church endeavor to do for one of its members whom God has called to be a missionary that would not be expected for another missionary *during deputation, while on furlough, while on the field and even after missionary service*?

CHAPTER 10: MISSIONS: WORLD EVANGELIZATION

6. What actions should be taken regarding missionaries that change from the field where they were deputized to serve and go to another field?

7. What should be done if a missionary resigns from one mission board or agency and joins another mission board or agency?

8. What policy should a church have for missionaries who have served for many years on the field but are no longer (*for one reason or another*) able to stay on the field?

9. When the church commissions one of its members as a missionary, is the commission for life (*with the exception of a doctrinal or moral disqualification*)?

10. When the church deputizes a missionary that is not a member of the church, is the commitment for life (*with the exception of a doctrinal or moral disqualification*)?

To have a written missions policy stating the church's _purpose_ and _policy_ has been determined to be necessary. With an approved written policy in place, no emotional decisions or decisions based on personalities will be involved in determining what the church will or will not do in any of these specific situations.

God gave the Great Commission to the local church. Each church must know what the New Testament teaches and what God would have the church do regarding worldwide missions and the missionaries that it supports. While specific answers may not be found in the Bible for some of the present day challenges, there are principles that help to address all the important and vital aspects of the ministry of worldwide missions.

Baptist International Missions, Inc.

PO Box 9, Harrison, TN 37341

Dr. Ray Thompson

A missionary closet can be a blessing to the church but especially to the missionary. A guiding principle concerning what items should be placed in the "closet" would be, "Give God choice, not charity." (Malachi 1:6-14)

There are at least three different plans for giving to missions:

1. The budget plan (A fixed amount that is part of the church budget)

2. The percentage plan (A percentage of the total offerings for the year are given to missions – that is, 10%, 15%, 50%, etc.)

3. The faith promise plan (The members are encouraged to give a set amount each week, month or year above their regular tithes and offerings to missions). **This is a God honored plan and by faith brings God's resources into the mission's budget of the church.** It stretches the faith of the believer and brings in funds above the regular offerings of the church. God honors faith.

Considerations:

1. It usually is wiser to support several missionaries for a lesser amount (For example, ten at $50.00 a month, or five at $100.00 a month as opposed to one at $500.00... unless the missionary is a member of the church). The

average monthly support in 1997 was $50.00 a month. It would be better if it were $100.00 a month. The missionary would have fewer churches to contact to raise his support and also when on furlough.

2. Of mission's money available, some could be set aside for pastor's yearly missions trip, emergencies, or special projects. The major portion should be reserved for monthly missionary support.

3. Missionaries sent from the church should receive special attention and greater support.

Note:

An article written to encourage and offer some suggestions to "sending churches."

THE SENDING CHURCH ...

Baptist International Missions, Inc. requires that each missionary with BIMI be sent out by a local independent Baptist Church. The role of the sending church is primary, vital and above all, biblical. BIMI respects the biblical order in the chain of authority to which each missionary is accountable. BIMI as a missions agency does not pretend to usurp the authority or take the place of the local church. BIMI was established as a "handmaiden" to serve and assist the local sending church, sending pastor and the missionary.

Blessed is the local church that has the privilege of serving as "sending church" for missionaries called forth from its congregation. The sending church and pastor have great opportunities as well as responsibilities. The missionary who recognizes God's order and provision will value the ministry and role of the sending church and pastor in his life and ministry. He will strive to maintain the proper relationship with his sending church and pastor. At BIMI we encourage this constantly.

In BIMI's Candidate School, the new missionaries are instructed to avoid situations that would cause them to seek approval or permission from their sending pastor to do something that conflicts with accepted policy. Policy has been established by the Pastors that make up the Board of Trustees to assure order and accountability. By signing the BIMI application form, each BIMI missionary agrees to abide by these policies. Applicants are encouraged to give serious prayerful consideration to the BIMI standards, doctrinal statement, and policies, before signing and submitting the application.

The world in which we live is very different from the world in which the Apostles lived and served. There was basically only one government with which they had to deal, the Roman government. There are over 200 foreign governments today. Each has its own set of laws and guidelines for issuing visas, residence documents, etc. Most have a unique currency, culture, idiom, and even restrictions on religious activity. Mission agencies are generally able to assist churches and missionaries in dealing with these variables.

In the first century the missionaries were only accountable to a handful of local churches in Antioch and Macedonia, etc. There were few missionaries. Today there are thousands of missionaries and tens of thousands of churches around the world. Most missionaries have 50-70 supporting churches. Each of these churches has the right to expect a certain level of accountability from the missionary. The policies of BIMI and other fundamental agencies respect the sending church as the final institutional authority in the life

CHAPTER 10: MISSIONS: WORLD EVANGELIZATION

of the missionary but also provide for the accountability that each supporting church expects.

SUGGESTIONS FOR THE SENDING CHURCH:

<u>Pray for your missionaries daily.</u> Pray specifically for their personal and ministerial needs. Keep their names before the members of the church continually for prayer.

1. Pray for their personal growth, for their safety and for them to have good results as they serve Him.

2. Pray for their pre-field ministry (deputation). Pray for open doors to present their passion for souls and the field of service in potential supporting churches. Pray they will see souls saved and be a blessing in these churches. Pray the Lord will touch hearts so that the needed prayer and financial support will be acquired.

3. Pray for their family, for the wife, for the children, etc.

4. For safety as they travel.

5. For their health.

6. For their needs to be met.

7. Pray for the missionary's **heart,** his **home**, his **helpers**, his **health,** for **help** financially, to be able to **overcome hindrances**, for **holiness**, for his **times of heaviness** and especially for the **harvest of souls**.

<u>Be involved as much as is possible in their ministry.</u>

1. Make missionaries that are members of your church a special concern and treasured blessing.

THE BASICS OF CHURCH PLANTING

2. Help them more, intentionally and specifically, than the non-member missionaries you support.

   a. Support them monthly for more than you do most missionaries, if possible. Some sending churches support their own missionaries with an amount equal to 10% - 20% of the total amount of monthly support needed. Some sending churches support their members with a set amount such as $300, $400, or $500 a month. Many times these amounts are more than covered by the extra that missionary's family members want to give to them through the church. This may not be practical, in the immediate future, for sending churches that have a large number of members that are missionaries. It could be a long-term goal.

   b. Help them with the costs of Candidate School or the expenses of a survey trip to the field.

   c. Help them with special offerings for equipment... a computer and projector for their multi-media presentation, the first printing of prayer cards, the cost of brochures, the cost of postage for their mailings, etc. Since the missionary will not necessarily need the projection equipment once they leave for the field it could be available "on lend". This arrangement might allow several missionaries to benefit from the same equipment.

   d. Help them get started on deputation by providing them with a travel vehicle, the use of a mission house or apartment, an office phone or prepaid phone cards, by placing them on the church's health insurance plan or even a minimal salary for the first few months of deputation so they can

CHAPTER 10: MISSIONS: WORLD EVANGELIZATION

      work fulltime at the deputation ministry, etc. <u>Not all churches will be able to do all of these things but anything the sending church is willing and able to do, by God's provision, will be a blessing to the missionary and the church (Acts 20:35).</u>

3. Other things that can be done…

   a. **Write a letter of recommendation** for them or give a brief recorded statement for their multimedia presentation.

   b. **Make phone calls or write letters to fellow pastors** suggesting they allow your missionary family for a meeting to present their field and ministry or invite them to attend their annual missions conference. The sending pastor, because he is known and respected by other pastors, can be greatly used of God to help the missionary schedule meetings.

   c. Help them with baby-sitting when needed.

   d. Ask them from time to time how things are going. Make sure they are not doing too much. Require accountability. Encourage family time.

   e. Be a friend to them

   f. Counsel them concerning preparation for the field.

   g. Have a "commissioning service" before they leave for the field.

   h. Remember the missionary family's birthdays, anniversary, and at special times during the year (Christmas, Easter, Fourth of July, etc.).

i. Send tapes or videos of the church services, the church bulletin, etc. Check with the missionary before sending packages.

j. Have a special section in the church directory for the missionaries sent from your church. Post addresses (email and otherwise), phone numbers, etc., if appropriate.

k. Post their prayer letter in a special place, print the letter in the church bulletin, etc.

l. Arrange for the pastor to visit them on the field.

m. Provide or help arrange for housing, transportation and other needs when they come on furlough.

n. Maintain an open line of communication with the mission agency. Inform the mission agency of potential problems or of areas in which it can be of help.

Again, I remind you that these are only generic suggestions. Not all of them will be relevant or practical for every church. **Many churches have superbly organized and well developed missions programs.**

The field is ripe unto harvest. May the Lord Jesus Christ bless so that your missionaries can soon be ministering on the field to which God is leading them.

The church planter will have the great privilege of guiding his people into a Christ-honoring missions program.

Note:

On the foreign field and especially in what are known as two-thirds world countries (under-developed) the church planter will need to teach the people the grace of giving to missions as presented in II Corinthians Chapters 8 and 9. There also is the need to help the established churches ban together to form a national missions agency through which national funds and missionaries can be sent to the field. The establishment of national agencies will facilitate the accountability necessary for nationals to raise a portion of the needed support in the USA.

A Suggested Missionary Policy

(The following missionary policy can be adopted by the church at the recommendation of your missionary committee.)

I. Missions Philosophy

   A. The Missionary and his work:

   The missionary is a Spirit–called individual used in the fulfillment of the Great Commission. The local church is the agent God uses to commission or send the missionary to the mission field. The mission agency is that organization directed by God for the purpose of assisting the local church in the administration of the mission's ministry.

   B. Extension of the local church:

   A local church, by nature, is in a permanent location. Any missionary supported by the church is considered to be an extension of that ministry. The missionary will be requested to subscribe to the Statement of Faith and attest to his agreement with the position of the church.

C. Church planting/evangelism extension:

    Believing that the winning of souls is not the complete fulfillment of the Great Commission, the missionary should also view as important the establishment of local indigenous churches, based on the Word of God.

II. Missions Committee

    The primary function of the missions committee will be to carry out the missions policy of the local church, including responsibility for the annual missionary conference. Its overall objective is to encourage all church members to become more actively involved in missions.

III. Missions Program

  A. Balance

    Missions is a worldwide responsibility of the local church and should be balanced in regard to:

    1. General and Special

    Since there is no Biblical substantiation for specialization in the missionary endeavor, a missionary supported by this church shall be primarily involved in general missionary outreach.

    2. Home and foreign

    Believing that the witness is to be borne in "Jerusalem, Judea, Samaria, and unto the uttermost parts of the world," home missions is to be deemed necessary and of equal importance with foreign missions.

CHAPTER 10: MISSIONS: WORLD EVANGELIZATION

B. Mission Agencies:

This church will support only missionaries serving with a Baptist agency whose doctrine is in conformity to the Statement of Faith of the church.

C. Candidates:

Candidates for support shall be interviewed by the missions committee. They should be willing to answer questions that the committee considers essential for the evaluation of their ministry.

1. Frequency

Candidates will not exceed four in number during the course of a year, preferably one a quarter (including the missionary conference).

2. Selection for recommendations to the church

Candidates will be interviewed by the missions committee before recommendation to the church for support.

3. Members of the church

Members of this church appointed by approved mission agencies shall be supported at a higher level: (amount).

D. Finances:

Faith Missions calls for faith in the provision of God for the needs of those who have been called to minister the gospel. The fact that missionaries need support does not indicate a lack of faith on their behalf, but is in keeping with the faith principle.

1. Honorariums

    Special offerings will be taken for missionaries who present their work or report to the congregation. Honorariums should be at least $50.00 plus expenses, with cash being given to the missionary if there is a present need.

2. Support levels, minimums

    No missionary will be supported for more than 40% of his or her total support. The minimum support will be ($50.00, $75.00, or $100.00) per month.

3. Retirement, support for retirees

    Missionaries will be urged to include in their support planning an amount that will be designated as retirement fund. The committee suggests $50.00 per month minimum for this purpose. The missions committee will interview each retiree to determine his or her retirement needs. If a need is evident, then the committee will recommend continued support up to 50% of that which had been received during the active ministry.

E. Prayer:

Prayer is the church's intercessory ministry for the missionary on the field. The missionary as well should be encouraged to remember the supporting church in prayer.

1. Monthly bulletin

    Each missionary letter received will be excerpted and given to each member of the church in a monthly prayer-request bulletin. This should be distributed as soon as possible after the first Sunday of the month.

CHAPTER 10: MISSIONS: WORLD EVANGELIZATION

    2. Emergency requests

        As information is received concerning emergencies, the committee should notify the entire church. The church should handle any monetary needs as quickly as possible.

  F. Women's Missionary Fellowship:

      Women's Missionary Fellowship will be an adjunct of the total missions program of the church. Women's Missionary Fellowship will continue to supply such work and needs as set forth in the constitution. It will be responsible to maintain a missionary cupboard, which will help meet the needs of the missionaries. The entire church should be advised of needs for the missionary cupboard and be encouraged to participate in this ministry.

  G. Missions and Satellite Churches:

      In the event a satellite church is started or a local mission is established, the missions committee would encourage members of the church to become personally involved in them, even to joining these works in the formative years.

IV.   Missionary Personnel

  A. Communication:

      It shall be the responsibility of missionaries to keep the church informed (at least quarterly) as to the progress of their work, including special items, both for prayer and praise. Should there be any proposed change of ministry, i.e. country, organization, etc.; the church is to be notified by the missionary as soon as possible.

  B. Interview and evaluation of ministry:

Prior to the missionary's return to the field, he or she should meet with the committee to reaffirm his or her commitment to the church's Statement of Faith. The missionary shall also provide a personal testimony and answer any questions that the committee may have.

C. Withdrawal of support and reinstatement:

The decision to recommend support withdrawal of a missionary rests with the missions committee. Reinstatement will follow the same policy as for new missionaries.

D. Furlough responsibilities:

Each missionary shall contact the church in the year prior to furlough so that the scheduling of meetings can be arranged as far in advance as possible. Hopefully this will permit the missionaries to participate in VBS and the annual missionary conference.

A Suggested List of Items for the Missionary Closet

Linens: Pillow cases, sheets, quilts, blankets, bath towels, washcloths, bedspreads, tablecloths, dish towels, aprons, doilies, dresser scarf's, yard goods for curtains and drapes, crochet or braided rugs, pot holders.

Toiletries: Toothpaste, soap, Kleenex, deodorants, hair tonic, combs, shampoos, toothbrushes, toilet

CHAPTER 10: MISSIONS: WORLD EVANGELIZATION

	paper, powders, razor blades, aftershave lotion.
Tupperware:	Most types of plastic covered dishes or containers.
Paper items:	Cups, plates, napkins, wax paper, aluminum foil, Saran wrap, paper towels, handy-wipes, copier paper, stationery, greeting cards, thank you notes, envelopes.
Teaching Aids:	Crayons, glue, scotch tape, masking tape, pens, pencils, marking pens, paper punches, stapler and staples, hi-liters, rubber bands, construction paper, carbon paper, stencils, flashcard stories, illustrated songs, easels, flannel graph stories.
Sewing supplies:	Yard goods, tape measures, thread, needles, pins, snaps, hooks, pincushions, scissors, sewing patterns.
Tools:	Hammers, pliers, wrenches, assorted nuts and bolts, screwdrivers, tape measures, high-speed drill bits, electric drill, sand-paper, wood glue, clamps, heavy-duty extension cords, paint brushes, hacksaws, hand saws, squares, chisels, batteries, flashlights, stud finders, files, jumper cables.

Other Items: Pre-paid telephone cards, pre-paid gas cards, postage stamps.

** All items placed in the missionary closet should be new and unused.

** Please <u>leave the price tags on your items</u> so the proper point value can be placed on it (one point for each 25 cents). The price tag will be removed when the point value is placed on it.

** Look for sale items to s-t-r-e-t-c-h your missionary dollar.

FAITH PROMISE OFFERINGS FOR WORLD EVANGELIZATION

In His last words before His ascension to heaven Jesus said:

"Go ye, therefore, and teach all nations, baptizing them in the name of the Father, and of the Son, and of the Holy Ghost: Teaching them to observe all things whatsoever I have commanded you: and, lo, I am with you always, even unto the end of the world. Amen." Matthew 28:19-20

In another place He said:

"...Lift up your eyes, and look on the fields; for they are white already to harvest." John 4:35

THE **COMMAND** IS CLEAR. THE **NEED** IS OBVIOUS

The **FAITH PROMISE PLAN** of giving answers the need:

➤ It provides more money for missions

CHAPTER 10: MISSIONS: WORLD EVANGELIZATION

- It enables churches to send more missionaries
- It involves individual believers in the program of world evangelization
- It brings "faith in God" into the equation.
- It taps into God's resources (Phil. 4:19)

HERE'S HOW FAITH PROMISE GIVING WORKS:

1. FAITH PROMISE cards are distributed to each person.
2. They prayerfully consider how much they are willing to trust the Lord to enable them to give to missions above their tithes.
3. They fill in the amount of their FAITH PROMISE OFFERING and turn in the card.
4. The church totals all the cards and promises missionary support based on the total FAITH PROMISE OFFERING of the people.
5. Week by week the believers give their FAITH PROMISE OFFERINGS as God prospers them and enables them to give.

This is nothing new for the church, except that their missionary commitments were based on tithes before. The church still made a faith commitment, since the amount of tithes is as uncertain as attendance, job security, health, and many other variables.

THE BLESSINGS ARE ABUNDANT

1. God is glorified as He provides both the gift and the needs of the believers and the church in fulfillment of His promises.
2. Missionary's support needs are met enabling them to go forth with the gospel.

3. The local church is enabled to carry out the Great commission more effectively.

4. The Lord meets the needs of individual believers. (Matthew 6:33)

5. The Lord meets the collective needs of the local church. (Philippians 4:19)

The FAITH PROMISE PLAN of missionary giving is based squarely on the biblical plan of faith in action and, therefore, it works and is attended by God's blessings.

WHY SHOULD I MAKE A FAITH PROMISE OFFERING?

Some biblical reasons for making a Faith Promise Offering.

1. **To prove or demonstrate my love for God.** "I speak not by commandment, but...to prove the sincerity of your love." (2 Corinthians 8:8)

2. **To help with the carrying out of the Great Commission.** The last commandment of Jesus was to evangelize the entire world (Mathew 28:19, 20). This is yet to be fulfilled. All of us who are Christ's disciples are responsible for its fulfillment. Missionaries are desperately trying to raise their support so they can go to their fields. My faith Promise Offering will help provide the money with which to send them. *"And how shall they preach except they be sent?"* (Romans 10:15)

3. **To put faith into practice.** "For we walk by faith, not by sight." (2 Corinthians 5:7); *"...so faith without works is dead also."* (James 2:26)

4. **To abound in the grace of giving.** *"Therefore, as ye abound in everything...see that ye abound in this grace also."* (2 Corinthians 8:7)

5. **To follow the many biblical examples of faith giving,** e.g., the widow of Zarephath (1 Kings 17:8-16); the Macedonian Christians. (2 Corinthians 8:7)

CHAPTER 10: MISSIONS: WORLD EVANGELIZATION

6. **To follow the example of the Lord Jesus Christ in giving.** *"For ye know the grace of our Lord Jesus Christ..."* (2 Corinthians 8:9)

7. **To follow the inspired advice of Paul** who said it is expedient, not only to give, but to make a commitment to give. *"...for this is expedient for you..."* (2 Corinthians 8:10)

8. **To experience the blessings of the Lord Jesus,** who said, *"It is more blessed to give than to receive."* (Acts 20:35). Cf. Also Luke 6:38

9. **To encourage others in the grace of giving.** *"...and your zeal hath provoked very many."* (2 Corinthians 9:2)

10. **To reap a bountiful spiritual harvest in my own life.** *"But this I say, He which soweth sparingly shall reap also sparingly; and he which soweth bountifully shall rap also bountifully."* (2 Corinthians 9:6)

11. **To experience the love of God in all its fullness.** *"...for God loveth a cheerful (hilarious) giver."* (2 Corinthians 9:7)

12. **To prove God and thus build my faith.** *"Prove me now herewith, saith the Lord of hosts..."* (Malachi 3:10)

13. **To bring glory to God.** *"Whiles by the experiment of this ministration they glorify God for your professed subjection unto the gospel of Christ, and for your liberal distribution unto them, and unto all men."* (2 Corinthians 9:13)

14. **To build up my account in heaven.** *"But lay up for yourselves treasures in heaven..."* (Matthew 6:20). *"Not because I desire a gift: but I desire fruit that may abound to your account."* (Philippians 4:17).

15. **To please God.** *"...an odour of a sweet smell, a sacrifice acceptable, well-pleasing to God."* (Philippians 4:18)

SAMPLE FAITH PROMISE CARD

****

FAITH PROMISE

A Faith promise is an opportunity for Christians to give as God has blessed them for the support of missionaries. This is an opportunity to be used of God to give to missions what you believe He will supply. The person making this faith promise is saying, "Lord, I will give to the missions program of (____name of the church____) as You make it possible."

"EVERY MAN ACCORDING AS HE PURPOSETH IN HIS HEART, SO LET HIM GIVE..." 2 CORINTHIANS 9:7

MY FAITH PROMISE GIVING:

Believing God will supply, I want to help support missionaries around the world that preach the Gospel message of redemption in Christ, by trusting God for the following (amount) each (time period) for the next 12 months, or a total of (amount) for this coming year.

Our prayer is to increase our missionary giving to $____.00 per week. This will make it possible for our church to be actively and directly involved with worldwide missions.

CHAPTER 10: MISSIONS: WORLD EVANGELIZATION

HOSPITALITY AND MISSIONS

by Faithway Baptist Church

Condensed and reprinted with permission from The Servant's Scroll

We should go out of our way to minister and encourage those who are serving the Lord. There is nothing special about the person; however, the office is something the Lord does exalt. Therefore, we ought to give heed to the Scripture and understand the principles regarding hospitality and missions. Before we see some hospitality helps in III John, let me share a couple of foundational truths.

1. A Gift To The Church

Ephesians 4:11 says, "And he gave some apostles; and some, prophets; and some evangelist; and some, pastors and teachers." The reason they were given is in verse 12 – "For the perfecting of the saints, for the work of the ministry, for the edifying of the body of Christ." Without going into too much detail, let me say that the gift of the prophet and the gift of the apostle, in the sense that they are mentioned here, have passed. The apostles and prophets were foundational to the church ministry. The gifts remaining for the church today are the next two. The Bible says, "...and God gave...some evangelists, and some pastors and teachers."

The gift of pastor and teacher is one in the same. The gift of evangelist precedes the gift of pastor/teacher. The evangelist in the New Testament was not a man who came into town with his fifth wheel, showed up at a church from Sunday to Friday, and held evangelistic meetings. The evangelist in the New Testament was the church planter – the man who would travel into an area where Jesus Christ had not been preached. In that place he would preach Christ and win people to the Lord. They would be scripturally baptized and discipled, forming a New Testament church.

The evangelist today is the missionary – a church planter. The evangelist-missionary then is first and foremost on God's list! I have often said, "You can't have a pastor without an evangelist-missionary unless that pastor was first an evangelist-missionary." Somebody had to start the church. An evangelist-missionary, sent by a local church, had to go and lay the groundwork and win those people to Christ. Somebody had to disciple them. The pastor then comes and carries on his ministry of preaching, teaching, and perfecting. The Bible says, "...perfecting the saints, for the work of the ministry." This means equipping the church to serve the Lord.

I want you to understand as a foundational truth – the missionary-evangelist is a gift to the church! We need all of them, commissioned from their local churches, so churches can be started all over this country, and all over the world.

2. Esteem Them Highly

1 Thessalonians 5:12, 13 say, "And we beseech you, brethren, to know them which labour among you, and are over you in the Lord, and admonish you; and to esteem them very highly in love for their work's sake. And be at peace among yourselves." Paul says, "Know those people who are labouring among you." Not know about them, but know them. The labour that he is talking about is a spiritual labour. The church planter and the one that comes along and perfects that group to continue doing the work of the ministry are to be esteemed. The Bible says in verse 13, "...esteem them very highly in love for their work's sake." It does not say, "Esteem them high in love because you relate with their personality," or, "Esteem them very highly in love because you get along with them well and you have so much in common." The Bible says, "Esteem them highly in love for their <u>work's sake</u>." When we talk about hospitality and missions, we are talking about something biblical. "Lift them up," the Bible says, "Because of the work that they are doing."

3. Share Material Things

Galatians 6:6 – "Let him that is taught in the word communicate unto him that teacheth in all good things." We ought to communicate material things to the one that teaches spiritual things.

CHAPTER 10: MISSIONS: WORLD EVANGELIZATION

Let's keep it in context – verses 7-10, "Be not deceived; God is not mocked; for whatsoever a man soweth, that shall he also reap. For he that soweth to his flesh shall of the flesh reap corruption; but he that soweth to the Spirit shall of the Spirit reap life everlasting. And let us not be weary in well doing: for in due season we shall reap, if we faint not. As we have therefore opportunity, let us do good unto all men, especially unto them who are of the household of faith." Paul is saying to churches in Galatia, remember those who are communicating the Word to you. Communicate unto them. Look after their needs. In the context, Paul is talking about distributing – showing hospitality and esteeming those that are church planting, preaching and teaching.

The subject of hospitality and missions is rooted in the Scripture. It is something we all ought to be involved in – pastor and people. Everybody ought to take it upon himself to be hospitable to those serving the Lord.

I have heard a few horror stories of missionaries showing up at a church and spending the night in a Sunday school classroom. Old army-type cots were placed there for the family to have a good night's rest, while the members of the church endured the evening hours on comfortable beds. I have heard where church planters have traveled and ministered, only to leave without receiving a sufficient love offering or honorarium to cover expenses. Sometimes we just don't think in advance. We ought to err on giving too much instead of giving too little!

With these foundational truths in mind, let's focus on III John. This epistle gives us the testimony of a man named Gaius and his hospitality to visiting missionaries. Gaius took very seriously the opportunity to be a blessing to a servant of the Lord. We ought to learn from this example and implement these things into our personal lives and local churches.

The Participation of Hospitality

If we have a missionary in our church, it is obvious not everybody can have them in his home. However, everybody can participate in hospitality to some degree.

We have missionaries in our church on a regular basis. I also have the opportunity to be involved in missions conferences. I am amazed at the ways guest missionaries are ignored or taken for granted. We ought never to walk by the missionary standing by his display table and ignore him. We ought to speak personally to every guest servant of the Lord in our churches. We ought to meet his entire family. Many say, "Well, I'm just shy. I just couldn't." Learn to do it. We must get beyond ourselves and show hospitality to others.

In verse 5, John praises Gaius. "Beloved, thou doest faithfully..." Not the church corporately, but "thou" as an individual in the church. I am committed to this at our church. I want every missionary and special guest that comes to Faithway, to say, "This church knows how to make people feel at home. I have never been treated better!" It is the responsibility of every believer to show an interest in those who are serving the Lord. People have to be taught this today. Notice in that same verse John says, "...thou doest..." The word "doest" is a word that means an active labour – a process. To Gaius, hospitality wasn't just something that he thought about; it was something that he wanted to participate in.

The Persistence of Hospitality

Notice verse 5 – "Beloved, thou doest faithfully..." Gaius was not sporadic in his care for the brethren who came. He was faithful in his pursuit of making God's servants feel at home. Faithful believers who give of themselves to the Lord's workers are a great blessing. May our church be blessed with many who can be ready and willing to assist this way in the ministry.

The Parameters of Hospitality

Notice verse 5 once again. "Beloved, thou doest faithfully whatsoever..." I went to a church once that advertised, "We will treat you in so many different ways, you are bound to like at least one of them! We need to go out of our way to be a blessing. Love offerings are an important necessity to the missionaries, but there are other things that are important as well. Little things can mean a whole lot. Isn't it the small things you oftentimes remember? The small things may be a brief word or short note. Someone spoke to your heart, and you jotted a note down really quickly, and handed it to him after the service. He didn't even know you. Maybe he thought he had failed in his testimony, song, or message, but you really encouraged him. Maybe it was taking time to help with someone's children, or assisting with a vehicle need, a medical need, a clothing need, or in some other practical area.

The verse not only says "whatsoever" but it says, "thou doest to the brethren, and to strangers." This speaks of being equitable in our dealings. We all have our favorite friends, preachers, and missionaries. We know people that we feel more comfortable with, but the Scripture says to be kind hearted to the strangers. John is talking about those servants of the Lord that they did not know before they arrived at the church.

The parameters cover whatsoever and whosoever. Gaius was a living example of this type of hospitality. There was another man named Diotrephes in the church. He did not like what Gaius was doing and it appears that he wasn't happy about all of these strangers continually visiting the church. God deliver us from those that have the Diotrephes Disease! Let's expand our parameters in reaching out in helping and being a blessing to others. This is the way to experience the blessings of the Lord.

The Provision of Hospitality

The physical and ministry responsibility that we bear is a part of our hospitality. We take care of the people who come to minister to our church. We look after them. We feed them well. We give them enough money to get them on their journey so they can continue to work.

Notice what the Bible says concerning this in verse 6, "Which have borne witness of thy charity before the church." In other words, when they left that place, everybody was talking about Gaius: "If you ever get to go to that church, make sure that you ask to stay with Gaius. Make sure you get to go to his house. Make sure you have a meal with him. Make sure you get to meet his family."

THE BASICS OF CHURCH PLANTING

The Bible carries it a step further in verse 6, "...whom if thou bring forward on their journey after a godly sort, thou shalt do well." The phrase "bring forward" is the phrase we want to focus on. This phrase has many different meanings. It means "to escort; to conduct; to send forth; to bring out of one's journey; to aid in travel." In other words, we ought to help fit the servant of the Lord with the requisites necessary to get the job done. This thought is expressed many times.

Genesis 18:16 – "And the men rose up from thence, and looked toward Sodom: and Abraham went with them <u>to bring them on the way</u>." Do you know who financed that trip? Abraham did.

Acts 15:3 – "And <u>being brought on their way by the church</u>, they passed through Phenice and Samaria, declaring the conversion of the Gentiles: and they caused great joy unto all the brethren." It was the church that provided for them so they could go on their way doing the work God had called them to do.

Acts 21:5 – "And when we had accomplished those days, we departed and went our way; and <u>they all brought us on our way</u>, with wives and children, till we were out of the city: and we kneeled down on the shore, and prayed." They saw them on their way and helped them continue on in the work God had called them to do.

1 Corinthians 16:5 & 6,

> *"Now I will come unto you when I shall pass through Macedonia; for I do pass through Macedonia. And it may be that I will abide, yea, and winter with you, that <u>ye may bring me on my journey</u> whithersoever I go."*

Paul knew they were going to help him in his ministry even to the point of lodging the entire winter there.

Romans 15:24 –

> *"Whensoever I take my journey into Spain, I will*

198

come to you: for I trust to see you in my journey, and <u>to be brought on my way thitherward by you</u>, if first I be somewhat filled with your company." Paul desired to go to Rome, and it would be those Christians who would make it possible.

Titus 3:13 –

"Bring Zenas the lawyer and Apollos on their journey diligently, <u>that nothing be wanting unto them</u>."

Paul says emphatically to look after their needs. He is saying to get them on their journey quickly and make sure their needs are supplied.

This ought to be our desire, attitude, and practice. May God give us many opportunities to help those serving the Lord and assist them in doing the work of the Lord. We want to fit them with the requisites necessary to carry on their ministry. The Bible promises if we do, "…thou shalt do well."

The Piety of Hospitality

The Bible says in this portion of Scripture, "…do it after a godly sort…," and, "…if you do it after a godly sort, thou shalt do well." John was trying to inspire Gaius to remember that he was treating those people – just like God treated them, and just like he would want to be treated by the Lord and by others. There is the quality of godliness when we give to others and care for them.

The Partnership Hospitality

Notice verse 7 of 3 John – "Because that for his name's sake they went forth, taking nothing of the Gentiles. We therefore ought to receive such…" There is something biblical about working together. Local churches sending and supporting those who are called is what it is all about. I say with John, "…we <u>ought</u> to receive such." This implies "to support"; "to welcome them"; "to bring them in"; "to provide for them." It actually carries with it the idea of lifting up, getting underneath them, and supporting them – welcoming them. This is a wonderful partnership. This is something we ought to do.

I remember in the earlier days of the ministry here, almost everybody who came in to minister here stayed with our family. Missionaries, guest preachers, those passing through, and so forth. They stayed for as long as they needed to. I remember one family stayed for a long time!

Thank the Lord as the church grows, more people are able to get involved. We now have people who are excited about having servants of the Lord in their homes. We also have some fine guest rooms to house full-time workers. I am convinced that we as churches and individuals reap in accordance to how we treat those whom God sends our way. If you want people in your church to reap blessings, get them to show hospitality to those serving the Lord. If you want your church to enjoy a measure of special blessing, bring in servants of the Lord and minister to their needs. Why should we do it? Look at verse 8 again – "…that we might be fellow helpers to the truth." We become fellow helpers by helping them.

This is what giving to missions and praying for our missionaries is all about. This is what opening your home is all about. This is what going back to a display table and taking a few minutes of your time is all about. You say, "I feel so uncomfortable." You have no idea how uncomfortable the missionary feels. He pulls into a strange parking lot, gets out of his car, and walks into a strange church. Maybe he has not met the pastor. He doesn't know what to expect. He sets up his display and wonders "Are they going to like me? Are they going to shun me? Are they going to be friendly? Am I going to get an offering? Are they going to respond to my preaching? Will they care for the people God has called me to reach? Will they pray for me? Am I going to get any financial support from this place?" YOU can make the difference in how they feel. YOU can become a fellow helper in the ministry.

Make sure you are a Gaius who loves those who love the Lord. Work at developing this attitude. Use it to inspire others and to promote the worth of the work of the ministry.

CHAPTER ELEVEN

THE FINANCES AND STEWARDSHIP PROGRAM OF THE LOCAL CHURCH

The expenses involved in planting a new church will vary from place to place. Rent and the cost of living in general are higher in metropolitan areas. Property or real estate will also be higher. The church planter should know ahead of time the costs that will be involved and be prepared. The initial, but also, continuing financial stability of the ministry will depend a great deal on the preparation and teaching of the church planter.

God's work is to be supported by God's people through "tithes and offerings." (Malachi 3:10, 2 Corinthians 8:8-9:15)

The church planter must teach his people to give at least 10% (the tithe or tenth part) of their income to the church. He should teach them that if they are going to "really give," they should give an amount above the tithe. The tithe belongs to the Lord, so we have not given to Him until we go beyond the tithe. The church planter can teach these truths from God's Word and by his example.

Note:

There are differing views concerning whether a missionary should remain as a member of his sending church, become a member of the church he is planting, or have some sort of duel membership. As a missionary church planter, he should work on the basis of duel membership. A pioneer church planter, who intends to remain as the permanent pastor of the church he is planting, could go ahead and move his membership to the new church. Unless arrangements are made with the new church, a church planter, who is not a member of the church, or any person for that matter, who is not a member, would not have legal right to vote in a church that is duly organized and incorporated.

There are also differing views concerning where the missionary or church planter is to give his tithe and offerings. Each person will have to have peace in his heart concerning this matter. If the missionary/church planter is to teach his people to give by example, then he will need to tithe to the church he is establishing. Once the church is established, it would seem unwise to encourage the members to send their tithe back to a church in another community from which they have come. This would seem to be the lesson taught if the church planter does not tithe to the church he is planting. A newly established church needs all the resources available.

If the missionary church planter is required to tithe to his sending church, the sending church might consider returning that amount to the missionary as an increase in monthly support.

I say again, each missionary church planter will need to settle this question with the Lord, his sending pastor and church.

A List of Financial Priorities Should Be Established

1. Monthly operating expenses (rent, lights, water, heat, repairs, literature, advertisements, etc.).

CHAPTER 11: THE FINANCES AND STEWARDSHIP PROGRAM

2. Pastor's salary and other staff members' salaries.

3. Missions Program (Missionary support, etc.).

4. Expansion expenses (building fund, property, etc.).

It will be necessary to keep these expenses before the people. Prayer should be offered. The members should be taught the stewardship principles found in God's word.

CONSIDERATIONS:

1. The church planter should train responsible people to assist in the handling of church funds. There should be duplicity and accountability so as to protect the testimony of the individuals and the church.

2. A practical, workable budget should be set forth and approved. Effort should be made to work within the framework of the budget.

3. There must be accurate records kept of all contributions, expenditures, and funds on hand (general fund, missions funds, savings, building fund, etc.).

4. The church planter may need to sign checks in the beginning especially, but even then it is best to have two signatures required on each check. Some church planter/pastors like to retain control of the checkbook. This may be necessary in some cases, but it is good to share this burden with responsible individuals and thus avoid what could be a source of doubt or criticism. The pastor who controls the check book and especially those who sign the checks alone open themselves up to unnecessary temptation and criticism.

5. Written financial reports should be made to the church on a regular basis. The financial program of the church should be characterized by honesty and openness.

6. All expenditures should be made by "check" when practical. The exception to this would be those made from the "petty cash" fund. The cancelled check serves as a receipt in addition to the normal receipts issued by the party to whom the check was made. Some churches use credit cards for certain expenditures. Again, receipts and controls are a must.

7. The budget should be reviewed annually (as a minimum) and appropriate adjustments or increases (pastor's salary, etc.) made.

8. Special Stewardship campaigns serve to challenge the members. They should be taught the principles of "living by faith' and presented with opportunities to stretch their faith. Stewardship begins with "giving ourselves to the Lord."

9. People should be taught and reminded that they, as well as all the resources God has placed at their disposition, belong to Him. We are only stewards. <u>The funds of the church are given by the members</u> of the church, and therefore<u>, they should have voice and vote</u> in how and for what expenditures are to be made.

CHAPTER TWELVE

THE CHURCH FACILITIES

This is one of the most important considerations of the church planting ministry. **Every church should have "adequate" facilities**. The definition of "adequate" will be determined by many factors. Some of these factors are as follows: location (city, suburb, country, jungle, etc.), the size of the congregation, projected growth, and the ministries of the church (Bible Institute, Day School; Orphanage, etc.).

Planning should be guided by the following:

1. **Real need and practicality**

   a. Is it adequate in size, number of rooms, etc?

   b. Is it accessible as far as location? Is it near most of the members or the community you wish to reach for Christ?

   c. Can the church afford it?

   d. Is it a wise decision? Is it in a flood zone? Are there liens, easements, restrictions, special zoning considerations, etc.?

   e. Are the neighbors desirable (bars, cantinas, next door to another church)?

Remember that real estate is generally an "appreciating commodity." You may invest in the beginning in a facility that is less than ideal but use it at a later date as collateral toward the purchase of a better facility.

2. Remembrance that the people are the "Church," not the building. The church planter's success in God's eyes will not be measured by how big the building is but how he has built the "Church", the body of Christ.

3. Constant awareness that we are only "pilgrims" passing through this world. (Titus 2:12-13).

"These all died in faith, not having received the promises, but having seen them afar off, and were persuaded of them, and embraced them, and confessed that they were strangers and pilgrims on earth." (Hebrews 11:13)

"By faith he sojourned in the land of promise, as in a strange country, dwelling in tabernacles... For he looked for a city which hath foundations, whose builder and maker is God." (Hebrews 11:9-10)

4. **The facility is "to be used" – not worshiped.**

"Where no oxen are, the crib is clean: but much increase is by the strength of the ox." (Proverbs 14:4)

The facility that is practical will get dirty. It can be cleaned. It will show wear. When it is worn, repair it. Some churches don't want to reach out to certain people (bus kids, etc.) because their facilities might get "messed up." God help them to see the error of their ways and the value of precious souls.

CHAPTER 12: THE CHURCH FACILITIES

Establish a "Building Fund" account

Set aside a portion of the weekly offerings for this fund. Have special fund raising drives. Encourage the people to give a regular amount above their tithes to the building fund. Generally speaking, a bank will not lend money to an individual or a church that does not have the discipline of "saving." Your building fund may serve as the down payment. It is so much easier to pay as you go and not borrow, unless absolutely necessary. Counsel yourself with men of God that have had successful building programs. If you are on a foreign field, talk with veteran missionaries, or counsel yourself with successful business-persons of confidence or in a village, with the chief.

DANGERS:

1. Presuming on the future and projected growth some "bond issues" are based on unreasonable growth projections.

2. A mistake made by many missionaries is to believe that people are too poor to build their own facilities. There are many examples of abandoned church buildings that were built by a missionary with U.S. funds. The people need to give and work to have their own building. Some assistance may be okay but the danger is to "do it all for them".

3. Seeking to keep up with the "Jones"

4. Building a "showcase" instead of a facility that is functional, adequate, etc.

5. Poor preparation and planning have led to many a "church split" in the middle of a building program. Decisions should be made beforehand about who will be involved (building committee, etc.) and how decisions regarding the construction of the facility are going to be made.

6. A building that "swallows" the congregation will be a disadvantage (i.e. heating or cooling unused space) for several reasons. A smaller, full building draws a crowd better than a huge building half full.

Note:

A church in a village of 250 inhabitants probably doesn't need a 500-seat auditorium.

7. A church should deal with a reputable and bonded contractor. Contracts should be clear, accurate, and binding. If work is to be done by the congregation, this should be defined clearly. A contractor that is a member of the church can serve as an advisor, but experience teaches that there are often misunderstandings and problems when using "in house" people. Unfair expectations are often the cause of these problems.

Note:

According to Paul and Luke in Acts 20:35, Jesus said, "It is more blessed to give than to receive."

If we do not teach and lead our people to give and support their total church ministry, (which includes supporting the pastor/s, supporting missionaries and, yes, building needed buildings) we are robbing them of the blessings of the Lord. Let us not cheat them out of God's blessing and provision. (Philippians 4:19)

CHAPTER THIRTEEN

PITFALLS OR DANGERS IN THE CHURCH PLANTING MINISTRY

In the beginning we suggested that the success or failure of the church planting ministry would be based upon the **PERSON** of the church planter. We are still convinced that this is true. The church planter should avoid the following pitfalls:

1. **Neglect in the matter of personal and family devotions**

    The ministry becomes mechanical if we neglect our daily quiet time with God. Stay in the Book and on your knees. In the matter of your personal devotions, read a chapter from an O.T. book, a Psalm, a Proverb, and a chapter from the New Testament each day.

2. **Neglect of family**

    Spend time with your family. Be considerate of your wife. Do not expect too much of your wife. You should see her as your wife and the mother to your children first. She will have her role to play in the church but don't expect her to function beyond her capabilities. **Your first responsibility is to your family.**

    "But if any provide not for his own, and especially for those of his own house, he has denied the faith, and is worse than an infidel." (1 Timothy 5:8)

Note:

You may say, "Yeh, I know, but I will never lose my family." Please believe me. If you do not practice Scriptural care for your wife and children you stand to lose them ... and your ministry.

To this very day church planters continue to neglect their wives and family and are having to leave the ministry as a result. It can happen to you. The enemy wants it to happen. Take at least a day a week just for your family. Do not be out "in the ministry" every night of the week.

3. Discouragement, Burnout, Success Syndrome, etc.

DISCOURAGEMENT

We have all had times of discouragement, as did many of the great men and women of the Bible (Numbers 11:15, Psalm 42:6, Jeremiah 15:10, Job 10:1). The problem comes when we do not deal with our discouragements face to face and overcome them through Scriptural means. Depression and defeat follow close on the heels of discouragement. Recognize that we are in a spiritual warfare (Ephesians 6:12). Take the armour God provides. Encourage your heart through God's Word.

Example: Read the story of Jehoshaphat in 2 Chronicles 19:1-25. Pay special attention to the size or number of things that could have discouraged him. Note his honesty as found in verse twelve. He also reminded himself of God's provision and deliverance on past occasions.

Though much depression may be the result of a chemical imbalance in one's body, much of the time depression is the result of un-confessed sin or an unforgiving spirit and

CHAPTER 13: THE PITFALLS (DANGERS) IN A PLANTING MINISTRY

failure to deal with offenses biblically. We must practice Scripture in these matters.

BURNOUT

Though there are many things that can lead to "burnout." A wise man will recognize his physical, mental, and emotional limitations and not push himself beyond them at least not on a continual basis. There is no dishonor or shame in this. The lack of caution in this matter often leads to depression, or what the world calls burnout. One consequence is "lost time" due to the need for recovery. Delegate and share your burdens with the leaders that you have trained. You are not big enough to carry the whole load by yourself. God doesn't intend for you to do so. Have a hobby. Take a family vacation. Plan activities that will refresh you and your family. Do not just plan them, do them.

THE SUCCESS SYNDROME

One of the greatest dangers of the church planter/pastor is to measure his success by "results." Many of us have been programmed to think that we are "okay" as long as we are "producing." When will we realize that "some water, others sow, and some reap?" We are to be **FAITHFUL**, but it is God who gives the increase.

Missionaries are especially susceptible to this malady. Supporting churches often expect "results" from missionaries that are unreasonable, results they don't expect from themselves.

Do not measure yourself by others. You are God's servant. You stand or fall according to His standard and His will.

4. **<u>Slothfulness (laziness, irresponsibility)</u>**

Because church planters are usually their own bosses, in a sense, it is easy to develop habits that are "time wasting." Plan your work and then work your plan. Develop a daily schedule. Stay busy (Proverbs 6:6; 24:30, 31, Ecclesiastes 10:18).

"Redeeming the time, because the days are evil." (Ephesians 5:16)

It is very easy for a missionary or pastor who has experienced a certain amount of success in his ministry to become careless. In the beginning when all depends on the missionary, he tends to spend a lot of time before the Lord in prayer. As others are won and trained and share his load, he tends to spend less time in communion with the Lord. This can very well open the door for serious temptation, temptations that lead to failure. We must beware!

Note:

David, once a success, became careless and neglectful of his duties as King of Israel. This "idleness" gave place to his sin with Bathsheba. All Christian workers should be on guard, especially once a certain amount of success in the ministry has been achieved.

(2 Samuel 11:1-12:14)

David "despised the work" given to him by God. God intended for David to be busy and an example as king.

The church planter has been given the great tasks of winning souls and planting the Lord's churches.

CHAPTER 13: THE PITFALLS (DANGERS) IN A PLANTING MINISTRY

David "despised the woman" with which he had sinned.

The man or woman of God that falls into sin with another person is evidently not concerned about that person's spiritual welfare.

David "despised the warrior" that faithfully served him.

The church planter/pastor can actually get to the place that he does not fully appreciate those that God has given to him as co-laborers.

David "despised the Word of God."

Nathan asked, "Wherefore hast thou despised the commandment

of the LORD, to do evil in his sight?"

We must do as Paul suggested in Acts 20:28 – "take heed unto ourselves."

5. <u>**Problems in the Church**</u>

The church planter must have discernment and foresight in the matter of problems. Problems must be dealt with in a biblical manner (Matthew 5:23, 24; 18:15-17 and I Corinthians 5). Problem people should not be received as members of the church unless they have the correct attitude and submissive spirit. If you know a person has caused problems elsewhere and receive them, you are only asking for trouble. It is better to have one person or family upset than to have them come in and influence several individuals or families. Don't ignore the problem hoping it will go away.

Pray about it and deal with it in an honest way. **If you have been wrong and have helped create the problem, admit it and ask forgiveness**. Have good lines of communication with your people. **Be honest, scriptural,** and, by all means, **keep things told to you in confidence and to yourself**.

CHAPTER FOURTEEN

THE FINISHED TASK: A NEW CHURCH PLANTED

There are three areas that we have already mentioned that are worth re-visiting.

- **Spiritual Maturity**

- **Numerical Maturity**

- **Financial Maturity**

These will all serve as indicators as to whether the church is ready to stand on its own and whether the missionary church planter can move on to another field. Even the church planter that intends to remain as resident pastor will need to strive for these three qualities.

There must be a level of **spiritual maturity in the lives of** the **members** of the church, but especially in those who are **leaders**.

There should be sufficient members to support the church and carry out its established ministry. There is no set number, but two or three people generally do not make up a congregation. There have been cases where two or three have had to hold a church together until the Lord sent a new pastor. On the foreign field, we generally sought to have 25-30 adult members before organizing a new church. The attendance usually grew to 75-100 before we would turn it over to a national pastor.

The number and quality of leaders was usually more important than total number of members.

The new church does not necessarily have to have finances to pay their pastor's salary, especially if he is willing to come as a part-time or bi-vocational pastor in the beginning. **The church does need to have financial stability, if at all possible** before the missionary church planter leaves.

Edward T. Hiscox's *New Directory for Baptist Churches* published in 1894, has long been the standard for Baptist polity. At the end of Hiscox's chapter on church officers, he adds seven notes, which are worthy of consideration by the church and pulpit committee. These seven points can be summarized as follows:

NOTES:

Note 1. Great care is needed in the selection of a pastor. Grave interests are committed to his charge, as the religious teacher, leader, and example for the flock. So vital an act should be preceded by earnest and protracted prayer for divine direction in the choice.

Note 2. In calling a man to the pastorate, the church should take deliberate care to know his record, what he has done elsewhere, and how he is esteemed and valued where he has previously lived and labored. A man of deep piety, thoroughly in love with the Word of God, is much to be preferred to the brilliant platform declaimer.

Note 3. If a young man without a record is called, his reputation for piety, sound sense and pulpit ability should be carefully considered. If he be of the right spirit and the right material, he will grow into larger

CHAPTER 14: THE FINISHED TASK: A NEW CHURCH PLANTED

usefulness through study, the endowment of the Spirit and the prayers of the people

Note 4. In giving a call, the church usually appoints a meeting for that express purpose, notice being publicly given two Sundays in succession. A Three-quarters vote of all-present at such a meeting should be deemed essential to a call. The candidate should be informed exactly how the vote stands, and what the feeling toward him is, concealing nothing. Let there be transparent honesty in so delicate and important a matter, and no deception practiced.

Note 5. The connection between pastor and people is sometimes made a specified and limited time. But more generally-now almost universally-for an indefinite time, to be dissolved at the option of either party, by giving three months' notice: or otherwise by mutual agreement. Permanency in this relation is greatly to be desired, as tending to the best good of all concerned.

Note 6. The too common practice of hearing many candidates preach on trial cannot be approved, and usually works evil to the church that indulges in it. A few sermons preached under such circumstances form no just criterion of a man's ministerial ability, pastoral qualifications, or personal worth.

Note 7. Is it right for one church to call a pastor away from another church? Merely to call a man would be neither wrong nor dishonorable. Let the responsibility rest with him of accepting or declining the call. But if one church should use other means to unsettle him by arguments, persuasions, and the offer of special inducements, it would be both unchristian and dishonorable.

If God has done a work and it is decided that it is, indeed, time for the church planter to move on to a new field then the church must call a pastor. The following are some guidelines that should help in this all-important matter.

The pulpit committee has the responsibility to recommend candidates to the church. Before such a recommendation is made, the committee should seek to learn as much as possible about the man. If he is pastoring a church, a member or a delegation from the pulpit committee may be sent to visit the church where he is preaching. This would provide an opportunity to observe not only his ability to handle the Word from the pulpit, but also the work that he has accomplished in his present location. The potential candidate may be invited to the church as a pulpit supply. Before recommending him to the church, the committee should have determined his position regarding

1. Doctrine. (Does he agree with and will he defend the doctrinal position of the church without mental reservation?)

2. Church covenant. (Has he read and does he agree with each covenant statement?)

3. Church constitution. (Has he read and does he concur with the constitution of the church?)

4. Will he continue the ministries of the church... missions, bus ministry, etc., or would he have a new agenda?

5. Spiritual gifts. (What does he consider his spiritual gifts, i.e. his strengths in the ministry?)

6. His family. (Does he have a biblical relationship with his wife and family? Are they in favor? (1 Timothy 3)

CHAPTER 14: THE FINISHED TASK: A NEW CHURCH PLANTED

7. Finances. (How does he handle his money? Is he prompt in paying his debts? Does he have any large indebtedness?)

8. Morals.

9. Does he meet the other qualifications of 1 Timothy 3:1ff?

10. Contemporary theological issues.

   a. Divorce and remarriage

   b. Charismatic movement

   c. Neo-evangelicalism

   d. Bible translations

   e. The Atonement

Only after the pulpit committee is satisfied that the man meets the qualifications should they recommend the church invite him as a candidate. It is suggested that the candidate and his family meet with the church for a weekend that is Friday through Sunday. The Friday-evening meeting would be more or less informal, a "get-acquainted" time, perhaps combined with a fellowship supper. Saturday would provide an opportunity for church families to invite the candidate and his family to their homes. The candidate should have maximum exposure on the Lord's Day. In addition to preaching in both services, he should teach the Adult Sunday School class.

The voting members of the church should meet with the candidate and his wife on Sunday afternoon or following the evening service. This will provide an opportunity for members to ask questions. It should be remembered that the candidate and his wife should also be accorded the privilege of asking questions of the church family. Not only does the church need to make a decision, but the candidate must also decide whether or not to accept a call if it is extended to him.

Candidates should not be viewed as competitors for a job vacancy. Consider only one candidate at a time. To vote on two candidates in one meeting could easily result in a church split. After the vote by the church, the candidate should be informed immediately whether or not he as been called by the church. If the call is in the affirmative, he should be provided with a letter stating the pastoral salary, vacation time and other benefits that have been discussed during the interview. If a candidate is rejected or refuses the call, the pulpit committee should seek another candidate in the same manner.

It is not the place of the church planter to call or install the new pastor. **His counsel should be sought and his opinion valued**, but it is the church's responsibility to call the new pastor. If the church planter has done his job well, he will be able to entrust this responsibility to his people.

Leaving a ministry is harder many times than starting a ministry.

The church planter must commend the people to the Lord. They all belong to him anyway.

"<u>Now to him that is of power to stablish you</u> according to my gospel, and according to the revelation of the mystery, which was kept secret since the world began, But now is made manifest, and by the scriptures of the prophets, <u>according to the commandment of the everlasting God, made known to all nations</u> for the obedience of faith: <u>To God only wise, be glory through Jesus</u>

Christ for ever. Amen." Romans 16:25-27

Remember:

Holy Ghost guidance is of essence.

The perimeters given in God's Word and summarized in our church documents guide us to faithfulness, consistency, and continuance in the faith, "the faith which was once delivered unto the saints." Jude 3

Closing remarks…

There is great need for fundamental, independent Baptist churches, men of God and their families to dedicate themselves to the task of planting new churches in America and around the world. The church planter will of necessity be a person of biblical faith, conviction, and perseverance. A pioneer spirit will be of great benefit to the church planter.

It is no easy task to begin a new church but the rewards are eternal. The church planter will think a hundred times that he is not gaining any ground but he must be faithful to the One that called him and the task He has assigned. Remember that the Lord Jesus Christ has promised to "build His church." **HE has and HE will.**

QUESTIONS – STUDY GUIDE

Chapter One

1. Where in the Scripture does the Lord Jesus Christ first promise to "build His Church"?

2. Approximately how many times is the word "ecclesia" used in the New Testament to refer to the universal church, the Body of Christ?

3. Approximately how many times is the Greek word "ecclesia" or "church" used in the New Testament to refer to a local assembly or congregation of believers?

4. What two terms are used interchangeably in the Scripture to refer to the action of beginning and establishment of new local churches?

5. Where in the four Gospels does Jesus give the "Great Commission" and what promise is given with each?

6. What is the ultimate goal of the church planter?

Chapter Two

1. What are the first two requirements concerning the "person" of the church planter?

2. What version of the Bible has God "preserved" for the English speaking world?

3. What must be the driving force in the life of the church planter?

QUESTIONS – STUDY GUIDE

4. What must the church planter be?

5. Name several areas in which the church planter needs to be stable.

6. In what ways should the church planter be prepared?

Chapter Three

1. What is the will of God for all believers?

2. What will be our practice if we follow the example of the Apostle Paul as expressed in Romans 15:20?

3. Into what three basic areas can the world be divided?

4. What three reasons for planting new churches in the metropolitan areas?

5. Church planting should be done for what primary reason?

6. What are three important factors when seeking a location (meeting place) in which to start and establish a new church?

Chapter Four

1. When considering "methods of church planting" what one factor should remain constant?

THE BASICS OF CHURCH PLANTING

2. What are three of the advantages of the "missionary church planter" method?

3. By what can the development of the church planting ministry of the "pioneer church planter" be slowed?

4. What are three of the advantages of the "sponsoring church" method?

5. Where or when is it possible that that the "sponsoring church" method may not be practical?

6. What should be considered by the individual that intends to spend his life as a church planter?

Chapter Five

1. What parts of the "Church Program" should the church planter prepare?

2. Name three important documents that the church planter should have prepared and on hand.

3. What literature should be prepared by the church planter?

4. After preparing a place where services can be held, what can be done?

5. In what should all preparation be bathed?

6. How can follow up be done?

QUESTIONS – STUDY GUIDE

Chapter Six

1. From what sources can the church planter find help so that his ministry is a team effort?

2. It is absolutely necessary for the church planter to do what?

3. What purpose do "get acquainted meetings" serve?

4. What are the keys for starting successfully?

5. In the "get acquainted meetings", after a brief gospel message, what should follow?

6. For a new church to be strong and established it must have what three things?

Chapter Seven

1. In depth teaching in what areas should precede the organization of the new church?

2. At this point what is extremely important?

3. What should be the basis for fellowship and unity in the new church?

4. Where might a church planter find a suitable Statement of Faith?

5. Which document sets forth the guide for administrative procedure by which the church functions?

6. Which document sets forth the doctrinal beliefs of the church as gleaned from the Bible?

Chapter Eight…Part One

1. Dr. Lee Roberson has often been known to say what concerning pastoral leadership?

2. What must the church planter provide at all times?

3. Setting goals allows the church planter to do what?

4. How can the church planter prepare for the regular business meetings of the new church?

5. Where are the qualifications of pastors and deacons found in the Scripture?

6. What should deacons always be?

Chapter Eight…Part Two

1. What should be set in the beginning of the new church?

2. Why is it important to "recruit" workers rather than ask for volunteers?

3. When working under the "team concept" what is necessary to delineate responsibilities?

4. What type of covenant can be prepared to insure "loyalty" from the church workers?

Chapter Eight…Part Three

1. What are the three key elements of the church service?

QUESTIONS – STUDY GUIDE

2. In what area of the ministry is it easy to grieve the Holy Spirit?

3. What are the two biblical ordinances of the local New Testament church?

4. In the matter of the Lord's Supper what should be noted?

5. What ministry of the church can be considered a ministry to parents having small children?

6. According to the Sunday School Worker's Covenant what responsibility does the teacher have to all visitors and absentees?

Chapter Eight…Part Four

1. The Sunday School can serve what two major purposes?

2. The church planter must provide doctrinally sound materials and do what with the Sunday School teachers?

3. For what should the Sunday School teacher have a burden?

4. What must be the relationship of the teacher and the Bible?

5. Who should be the "personal workers" of the church?

6. What is not too high a standard for church leaders?

Chapter Nine

1. When can it be said that the church planter has possibly finished his task?

2. Name three things that can be used to increase the missions vision of the pastor and church members.

3. What are the three most popular plans for giving to world missions?

4. What can facilitate the accountability necessary for national pastors and missionaries that would receive support from the USA?

5. What passage in II Corinthians can be used to teach "grace giving"?

6. What is the main purpose of a written mission's policy?

Chapter Ten

1. How is God's work to be supported financially?

2. Why are duplicity and accountability important in matters of finance?

3. By what should the church financial program of the church be characterized?

4. Why should the members of the local church be given voice and vote in the matter of expenditures?

5. What passage teaches that the tithe belongs to the Lord?

QUESTIONS – STUDY GUIDE

6. What arrangement might be made if the missionary church planter is required to tithe to his sending church?

Chapter Eleven

1. What should be the objective when seeking permanent facilities for the church?

2. What can be considered as an appreciating commodity?

3. Why is it important to remember to build people?

4. As soon as is practical what account should be established?

5. What mistake is made by many missionaries?

6. How do some missionary church planters seek to control new churches?

Chapter Twelve

1. What is the number one danger for church planters?

2. The first responsibility of the church planter is what?

3. What pitfall could be overcome by prayerful study of II Chronicles 19:1-25?

4. What can the church planter do to avoid "burnout"?

5. Ephesians 5:16 should be applied to the life of the church planter to avoid what sin?

THE BASICS OF CHURCH PLANTING

6. What four things did King David despise as he became lax in success?

Chapter Thirteen

1. What three types of maturity are needed if a new church to be considered established?

2. What should be preceded by earnest and protracted prayer for divine direction?

3. Before being recommended as a candidate for the pastorate the individual should define his position in what matters? Give four.

4. How many candidates should be considered at a time?

5. The church planter should do what to avoid "calling" the new pastor himself?

6. What is the last thing the church planter must do as he finishes his task?

RECOMMENDED READING:

Guided By Grace, Servant Leadership for the Local Church, by Dr. Paul Chappell, Published by The Sword of the Lord Publishers, 2000

Church Planting At The End Of The 20th Century, by Charles L. Chaney, Published by Tyndale.

Church Staff Administration, by Leonard E. Wedel, Published by Broadman Press.

Pastors At Risk, by H.B. London, Jr. and Neil B. Wiseman, Published by Victor Books.

Lectures To My Students, by C.H. Spurgeon, Published by Zondervan.

Indigenous Churches, The Goal of Biblical Missions, by Dr. Bob C. Green, Published by The Old paths Publications, Inc.

The Spiritual Leader, by Dr. Paul W. Chappell, ISBN 978-1-59894-052-7, Published by Striving Together Publications, Lancaster, CA 93535

Ephesians, Foundational Truths for Church Planters, by Dr David H. Snyder, Copyright 2008, Printed by Bible & Literature Missionary Foundation, Shelbyville, TN 37160

Issues In Missions Today by Dr. Les Frazier, Printed by Bible & Literature Missionary Foundation, Shelbyville, TN 37160

The Seven Laws of Teaching by John Milton Gregory, © 2006 Take Tenn Publications™, East Ridge, TN 37412

What The Bible Teaches About Drinking Wine by Dr Bruce lackey, Published by The Old Paths Publications, Inc.

Ten Ways To Study Your Bible by Dr. Bruce lackey, Published by The Old Paths Publications, Inc

INDEX

Acts, 4, 6, 9, 18, 19, 25-29, 31, 32, 34, 35, 38, 87, 90, 93, 97, 103, 114-116, 126, 133, 139, 141, 143, 155, 170, 179, 191, 198, 208, 213
Administration, 231
Advantages, 10, 58, 60, 63
America, 5, 16, 18, 41, 48, 51, 54, 82, 91, 135, 221, 239
Apostle, 18, 19, 28, 41, 46, 93, 223
Authority, 112
Baptists, 171
Bellue, 25, 27
Bible, 5, 6, 9, 21, 31, 42, 45, 54, 62, 67, 69, 71, 77, 80-82, 88, 89, 97, 98, 101, 103, 106, 108, 110, 112, 114, 117, 121, 139, 143, 144, 151, 152, 154, 160, 162, 168, 173, 193, 194, 197-199, 205, 210, 219, 222, 225, 227, 231, 232, 239
Bishops, 139
Body, 21, 112, 123, 222
Bride, 42
Build, 105
Building, 11, 13, 86, 207
Candidate, 176, 178
Chappell, 62, 133, 231
Charter, 11, 107
Christ, 6-8, 15, 16, 18-23, 25-27, 30, 32-35, 37, 40, 42, 44, 45, 47, 68, 79, 81, 86, 88, 90, 91, 93, 94, 95, 98-100, 107, 110, 112, 114-118, 121-124, 132, 140, 143-145, 148, 149, 153-156, 162, 166, 168, 169, 180, 190-194, 205, 206, 221, 222, 239
Church, 9-12, 21, 23, 27, 28, 30, 31, 42, 44, 49, 56, 58, 60-, 63, 65, 66, 82, 86, 100, 105, 107, 110, 115, 117, 124, 126, 127, 129-131, 133, 136, 153, 164, 172, 175, 182, 193, 206, 213, 218, 222-224, 231, 239
Church Planter, 10, 58, 60, 231
Cooley, 61
Corinthians, 19, 21-23, 26, 29, 33, 37, 40, 80, 89, 90, 94, 114-116, 145, 155, 156, 181, 190, 191, 198, 201, 213, 228
Council, 12, 129-131
Counsel, 179, 207
Covenant, 11, 12, 69, 110, 112, 118, 124, 130, 149, 162, 227
Cross-cultural, 43
Deacons, 139, 141, 142, 144, 167
Delegate, 211
Depression, 210
Deputation, 59
Disadvantages, 10, 59, 61, 64

233

Disciples, 6
Discourage, 157
Divorce, 219
Doctrine, 218
Edification, 11, 97, 151
Elders, 139
Ephesians, 4, 5, 21, 22, 29, 33, 42, 86, 90, 99, 114, 115, 133, 134, 193, 210, 212, 229, 231
Ethnic, 46
Example, 210
Faithful, 196
Father, 6, 22, 24, 25, 59, 76, 86, 114, 122, 154, 188
Fellowship, 106, 185
Field, 11, 16, 86, 105
Finances, 183, 219
Foundation, 231
Gaius, 195-197, 199, 200
Goal, 231
Gospel, 16, 35, 54, 80, 82, 117, 123, 192, 239
Grace, 62, 231
Great Commission, 16, 23, 88, 166, 173, 181, 182, 190, 222
Guidelines, 12, 145, 146, 157, 160
Heaven, 6, 122, 123
Hell, 123
Holy, 6-8, 19, 22, 24-26, 31-36, 38, 43, 46, 62, 73, 76, 86, 87, 90, 91, 93, 99, 102, 103, 110, 112, 114, 115, 118, 121-123, 133, 137, 141, 143, 149, 153, 154, 162, 169, 188, 221, 227
Holy Ghost, 6, 19, 24-26, 31-34, 38, 43, 46, 76, 86, 87, 90, 93, 137, 141, 154, 188, 221
Hospitality, 13, 193, 195-197, 199
Indigenous, 4, 9, 231
Institute, 6, 54, 205
Invitation, 156
Issues, 231
Job, 210
King James, 2, 31, 114, 122
Language, 27
Lead, 35, 168
Leaders, 11, 100
Leadership, 12, 35, 62, 149, 231
Leaven, 155
Liberty, 61
Local, 18, 62, 199, 231
Lord, 6, 7, 11, 19-24, 26, 28, 32, 34, 35, 40, 41, 44, 49, 51, 54, 57, 61, 62, 68, 73, 79, 80, 81, 85, 87-93, 99, 100, 102, 103, 107, 110, 112, 114, 115, 121-124, 132, 133, 137, 141, 142, 144, 151, 153, 154-157, 162, 163, 166, 177, 180, 189-202, 204, 208, 212, 215, 219-222, 227, 228, 231, 239
LORD, 9, 24, 26, 44, 48, 91, 213
Love, 33, 196
Matthew, 16, 19, 20, 21, 24, 26, 29, 32, 33, 42, 86, 88, 90,

INDEX

98, 99, 114-116, 121, 125, 166, 188, 190, 191, 213
Means, 121
Message, 131
Metropolitan, 45
Missionary, 10, 13, 58, 164, 165, 181, 185, 186, 189, 203, 231
New Testament, 4, 7-9, 18, 21-23, 28, 29, 71, 93, 106, 107, 112, 114, 115, 121, 136, 137, 153, 173, 193, 209, 222, 227
Nursery, 12, 157, 160, 164-166
Order, 84, 127, 139
Partner, 8
Peace, 25
Pentecost, 26, 27, 34
Philosophy, 181
Pioneer, 10, 60
Place, 156
Policy, 12, 13, 171, 172, 176, 181
Prayer, 12, 59, 130, 131, 149, 151, 162, 184, 203
Problems, 213
Property, 201
Purity, 31
Qualifications, 139
Rapture, 21
Record, 148
Roberson, 37, 66, 82, 132, 226
Romans, 18, 22, 28-30, 45, 68, 71, 95, 114, 115, 135, 148, 190, 198, 221, 223
Rural, 46
Saved, 54, 79
Scripture, 2, 20, 28, 38, 80, 91, 94, 99, 123, 131, 148, 151, 154, 170, 193, 195, 197, 199, 211, 222, 226
Service, 12, 119, 131, 162, 164
Son, 22, 24, 30, 53, 76, 86, 100, 114, 122, 154, 188
Soul winner, 91
Souls, 95
Staff, 231
Stewardship, 204
Study, 13, 68, 170, 222, 232
Suburban, 46, 47
Success, 13, 210, 211
Supper, 22, 115, 121, 123, 144, 155, 156, 227
Survey, 80
Task, 10, 65
Teacher, 91, 164
Thompson, 18, 171, 174
Train, 36, 68, 102, 146, 156
Training, 10, 11, 68, 100
Trust, 36, 101, 102
Truths, 231
Unity, 100
Visitation, 164
Voice, 136
Will, 51, 200, 218
Wine, 140, 232
Word, 5, 8, 19, 20, 25, 26, 30-32, 35, 37, 42, 67, 68, 99, 100, 103, 110, 111, 114, 117, 118, 121, 141, 142, 147, 162, 169,

182, 195, 201, 210, 213, 216, 218, 221
Workers, 12, 84, 146, 157, 164, 167
Worship, 10, 12, 49, 68, 151
Youth, 10, 69, 153, 164

ABOUT THE AUTHOR:

Bob Chapman Green was born in Fort Pierce, Florida on September 23, 1943, to Bob Clarence and Edris Marie Green. He accepted the Lord Jesus Christ as his Savior as a 12 year old boy attending Fairlawn Baptist Church. He surrendered to the Gospel Ministry when he was 16 years of age.

He graduated from Dan McCarty High School in 1961 and ultimately earned a B.A. degree with a major in Bible from Tennessee Temple College in Chattanooga, TN. He and Patsy Deitz were married in July of 1965. In 1967 they were approved as missionaries to serve with Baptist International Missions, Inc (BIMI) in Central America. They served as church-planting missionaries in Central America from August, 1968 until November, 1979. It was during those years that they gained much personal experience as church planters. They returned to the USA in 1979 because of the war in El Salvador.

During the past 40 plus years they have continued to serve with BIMI in various capacities. Though Brother Green has been a Director with BIMI, their main concern and passion has been for the ministry among Hispanics in the USA and some in Latin America. Church Planting has been a priority. Presently Dr. Green is Hispanic Ministries Representative and Aviation Ministries Director for the Mission. Brother Green has also written several additional books, including translations from English into Spanish.

The Greens have two children Susan Michelle Culler and Timothy Wayne Green. They also have six grandchildren (Danielle, Hunter, Logan, Natalie, Hannah (and Mitch) and Joshua (and Gabby), and two great grandchildren (Trevor and Brooklyn of Hannah and Mitch Feliciano).

www.ingramcontent.com/pod-product-compliance
Lightning Source LLC
Chambersburg PA
CBHW071711160426
43195CB00012B/1642